His Mistress

OR

God's Daughter?

Also by Danyelle Scroggins

The Strong Series

Destiny's Decision
Not Too Far Gone
Coming Soon
The Power Series

Standalone Titles

Not Until You're Ready
Coming Soon
Put It In Ink

The Jacobs Series

Evonta's Revenge

His Mistress

OR

God's Daughter?

DANYELLE
SCROGGINS

S&D
PUBLISHING

Unless otherwise indicated, Scriptures verses are from the taken King James Version of the Bible.
Scripture quotations marked (NIV) are taken from the Holy Bible, New International Version®, NIV®. Copyright © 1973, 1978, 1984 by Biblica, Inc.™ Used by permission of Zondervan. All rights reserved worldwide. www.zondervan.com

Published by:
Divinely Sown Publishing
4165 Monkhouse Drive Suite 111 Road
Shreveport, Louisiana 71109
www.divinelysownpublishing.com

HIS MISTRESS OR GOD'S DAUGHTER?
Copyright @ 2010 by Danyelle Scroggins.

ISBN-13: 978-0-9960038-4-1
ISBN-10: 0-9960038-4-3
Second Edition paperback November 2014
10 9 8 7 6 5 4 3 2 1

Printed in the United States of America
Book Design: Danyelle Scroggins
            www.danyellescroggins.com
Cover Model: Mrs. Tannie Bradley

Printed in the United States of America.

Dedication

This book is dedicated to my husband *Pastor Reynard Carter Scroggins Sr.* Thank you for always treating me like you married one of God's very own daughters. I love you with all of my heart and I will always remember.

Special Thanks to

My Mother *Helen S. Quaker Hall,* my Aunt Franklin James Phillips (Aunt Frankie), *Emma Yarborough Gatlin,* & *Lula Washington-* You've all been the perfect example of a wife and God's Daughters.

Thank you for teaching me how to love my husband and thanks for loving me!

"There is difference also between a wife and a virgin. The unmarried woman careth for the things of the Lord, that she may be holy both in body and in spirit: but she that is married careth for the things of the world, how she may please her husband."

1 Corinthians 7:34

Contents

Introduction

Why is it that it's so easy to pick out the type of woman you think with your heart of hearts is a mistress? We all have these preconceived notions of what a mistress is supposed to look like and how a mistress is supposed to act. We put up guards against the women who we think would become a mistress while the ones with the spirit of Jezebel run free and undetected. You can't bind or rebuke a spirit when you don't recognize it.

Let's take it to the church…

I've been in the church all my life and once Ms. Thang came strolling in, all the wives were wrapped around their husbands so tight until the brother couldn't hardly breathe. Don't act like you don't know what I'm talking about. We all know what Ms. Thang looks like. For those of you who act like you don't have a clue…. Here's a description of Ms. Thang. Ms. Thang has the latest trendy hair-do and it's styled to perfection. She has Mac packed on her face to exactness. She's most definitely a head turner in those stilettos that match perfectly with the ensemble she's chosen for morning worship that's fit for the club. The attitude of arrogance surrounds her like a halo and her designer vintage bag lets you in on the fact that she's not cheap. The exact prodigy of a Mistress walking but you could never be more wrong. Yes, sometimes this might be her description but not always.

His mistress doesn't always look like what you think she should look like. As a wife, you just would hope that if your husband is cheating, he'd find someone who looks better than you and is the total opposite of you. Ms. Thang often symbolizes the past you that he fell in love with; she embodies the way you use to dress, or act. So now that you know this, stop being so judgmental towards the women you think might be a mistress because what you think isn't always what's fact. In some cases, his mistress is more like you than you think and sometimes she possesses the qualities that you didn't think mattered anymore.

So, as you're trying to find out who she is and what she looks like, I'd like for you to remember that your commitment had nothing to do with her. She's lost in a world of her own and this is exactly why I'm writing this book. I've been silently watching so many of God's Daughters fall into forbidden relationships and what's even more painful...watching God's other Daughters fall victim to the pain that comes when another sister decides to be a mistress.

To those of you who are dealing with the struggle of safely enjoying being a mistress while neglecting the sacred position as God's Daughter, God has impressed upon my heart to let you know that it is far better being God's Daughter than a mistress. I know because regretfully, I've been on both sides of the coin. I can truthfully tell you that there was and is nothing man can give you that can top what God has in store for you as His Daughter.

You can't keep playing with God like this and He won't keep playing with you. This book is some of you all's last warning. God has been urging me to write this book. I wrote and finished it but the enemy was making things so crazy around me, until I prolonged getting it into yours hands. Your deliverance is riding on my life (literally), because if my disobedience causes your delayed deliverance, God will charge me. And after I have given you this to you and you fail to listen, you are no longer required on me.

If I don't put it out there for you to see, I will be held accountable. Why he chose me? Because I know how you feel. I know how it feels to be praying every day for God to send me a husband but to no avail. I know how it feels to see friends with husbands that they are cheating on, and all I wanted was a piece of husband. I know how it seems to feel lonely at night, when you pull down the covers and turn off the lights. I also know how Satan will manipulate you into giving yourself to a man that is not yours. So, who better to write this book than me?

Chapter One

When Lust Invades

Mandery

Mandery noticed that lately he'd become more aware of the women in his everyday surroundings...especially Sharmen Jones. She was his new secretary and she had it going on. He and his wife Christine had been married for over twelve years and although once happy, now they barely got along. He'd pride himself on being the husband of one woman and he enjoyed being Christine's husband before she got all caught up in their new found status. It's almost like the money was going to her head and the more she became hooked on the money, the more he became hooked on his secretary. Four months since he hired her and in the last two months, he'd been doing more butt watching than the law would allow.

Sharmen was a rather slender woman whose hips swayed easily from side to side when she walked. Her hair was always neatly pinned in a sophisticated up sweep and her face was always so radiant in the softest colors to match her outfits. Her eyes were dark and *mysterious and her lips were as luscious as a shiny Granny apple. Mandery had never desired another woman other than Christine, but his emotions were running wild where Sharmen was concerned. What was even stranger, she'd remind him of Christine when they first met.*

Something was truly happening to him and he wasn't sure if he wanted to fix it or let it be. He'd grown tired of Christine who was constantly running around town buying stuff to symbolize that she was married to the cream of the crop. It was apparent to him that Christine no longer used the possessions to enhance their lives, but now the possessions used her. Now all she seemed to be concerned about was getting more, having more, and looking like she was worth more. On the other hand, Sharmen was just your everyday around the way girl. She didn't change purses every time she wore different clothes. She often carried the same bag as if she appreciated being able to afford it. And this is what caught his eye.

The Virus…

So often in marriage we leave so many doors open for the enemy to come in. Think about a fly; as soon as you open your front door, they fly in fast. You had no warning that they were awaiting entrance and they move so fast until you can hardly catch them. We all know how dirty flies are and we would rather they not even come in. Because of their ability to fly in fast, you aren't quick enough to stop them from invading. I gave you that example so you can see just how LUST invades. It is a powerful spirit that moves quickly. It doesn't wait on you to welcome it in; it steals every opportunity through the opened doors of your heart and mind that you've neglected to close.

The enemy knows how to put the spirit of lust to work in our lives. He has three sources to infect you...the lust of the eyes, the lust of the flesh, and the pride of life. You would be surprised at the number of relationships and marriages that are built on these three infection carriers. Lust is just like a bad virus. It's an airborne infection that festers in air and is awaiting transfer; spirits are transferable. Like viruses, they find an open avenue to gain access into your body and then attach itself.

Think about this, viruses can only affect the fragile or weak immune system. It targets places where weaknesses have caused an infraction and it squeezes into a place where it can operate, grow, break-down, and make weaker. A virus is microscopic organism that causes disease and lust is an intense demonic spirit that produces sin.

Okay let's look at the machine everyone loves these days…the computer in contrast to the human. A computer can operate with a virus as long as it doesn't take full control; thus causing problems for the entire system. The objective of the virus is to plague the entire drive, stealing material, and eventually seizing and crashing the whole system. What's good is the system sometimes immediately starts showing signs that a virus is on board. It begins to operate slower and often the pop up material starts coming on the screen. Now if you don't do something to erase the virus, you'll allow it to strengthen. Although, you can pretend like it doesn't exist and only later find out that you'll need the help of a computer technician, to replace your entire hard drive. The stronger the virus gets, the harder it is to get rid of it.

Lust Can't Be Ignored

It's just like lust in humans....

A human can operate with lust but eventually lust will destroy the whole person.....physically, mentally, and spiritually. Lust is a spiritual virus and upon recognition that has invaded, you must take measures to get rid of it. Measures must be taken quickly and precisely because lust is evasive and perceptive. You can't get rid of lust by ignoring it or pretending that it doesn't exist in you. You have to admit that it is trying to attack you and prayer is now the responsive measure that you need to take. Prayer is your opportunity to invite your Creator in as your intercessor, helping you to rebuke and break the stronghold that lust is trying to put on you.

1 JOHN 1:9

"If we confess our sins, He is faithful and just to forgive us our sins and to cleanse us from all unrighteousness."

And yes, it is a sin that lust even had the opportunity to come in. How? I'm glad that you asked. Any crack that is unfilled is an open entrance to sin.

If you would have been prayed up and had your mind on the things of God, the enemy would not have had an opportunity to enter. When we allow lust to invade, initiate, and instruct in our lives we commit sin against our own bodies. Can't you see that it is vitally important that as soon as we recognize a moment's breakdown (a point in which we feel far from God or separated from His will) in our lives, we must repent, refocus, and renew our spirit man? If we ignore the virus (lust), we will give it ample opportunity to GO TO WORK!!!

Sharmen

Sharmen noticed how handsome Mandery was from the first day she interviewed with the firm. She'd also noticed the ring on his finger filled with huge diamonds that would be hard not to notice. She felt a strong attraction to him but had sort of sworn off men who belonged to other woman. Although she felt like she'd never have an opportunity to touch him, she couldn't resist sneaking a peak every now and again of his fine body.

Mandery was caramel brown with a mustache that connected to his beard with a thin line of hair on each side of his mouth. She had to admit that it made his handsome face, marvelous. His arms were big and strong and his smooth waves in deep black hair made him look like a fashion model on the beach. He was someone else's man, and daily Sharmen reminded herself of that. She'd made up in her mind that if he ever hit on her, she was going to give him just what he was looking for.

After a couple of months at the firm, she knew exactly when things weren't going right at home for him. Mandery had a certain twitch in his eyes when he was angry. Sharmen became more impressed with the *fact that he didn't allow his personal life to affect him at the office. She couldn't help being angry with his wife for making him angry. She tried relentlessly to hold in her feelings of discord but by the minute she was becoming more over-protective of him. She also had a very present thought that God always gave women who didn't need good men, good men.*

She'd started out praying a prayer of repentance when she thought lustful thoughts concerning Mandery. After he'd had a few more fights with his wife and the pain on his face was evident, she didn't care how morally wrong it was for her to be lusting after him. She envisioned herself as his wife. At least she was a working woman who wasn't caught up in stuff which was more than she could say for his wife.

JAMES 1: 13-15

13"Let no one say when he is tempted, "I am tempted by God"; for God cannot be tempted by evil, nor does He Himself tempt anyone. 14But each one is tempted when he is drawn away by his own desires and enticed. 15Then when desire has conceived, it gives birth to sin; and sin, when it is full-grown, brings forth death."

The Misguided Emotional Breakdown

When we allow our thoughts saturated in lust to fester, they soon take root. Then, the misguided emotional breakdown (when our soul is governed by emotion) causes us to believe that our feelings over-power the reality of what is morally correct. Eventually the brother of lust known as pride, steps into the picture. Once the brother comes to the playground, it is his purpose to make us feel that our wants trumps anything morally or spiritually correct. It is also pride's purpose to lie to us. Like….If God would have allowed him to find me first, we'd be married. He's the man God has for me. I can be the perfect wife for him. He needs a real woman and that's me.

I'm not saying that you aren't a real or good woman, but what I am saying is that the lie comes in when you feel you'll be best for him. In fact, if it had been God's will for you to have been with him, you would have. Pride understands that you (Christian women) know the Word of God and that you would rather follow God. Pride along with his two brothers: the lust of the eyes and the lust of the flesh are a threefold satanic trinity working against you. There's power in the three fold and Satan knows this. This is exactly why sin exists in three measures and why when these three brothers go to work, you soon go under fast and quick. They don't waste time working on your mind, the heart of your mind (thoughts), soul (which houses your emotions), and the most private interpersonal parts of your body. Their goal is to make you forget what you know is right and cause you to believe that you are right even though you are dead wrong. That's why people start trying to use the Word of God to justify their situations. I have found nothing more pitiful than a mistress trying to use God's word to validate her relationship with another woman's husband.

Can't you now see it? Then on top of all this, you have the same three demons going to work on the man you end up becoming a mistress to. Spirits are transferable and they recognize one another. Think about it, whether good or bad nothing just happens. Satan is constantly planting and orchestrating in our lives. He knows he's going down but he'll be dog gone if he goes down by himself. He already knows that he's going down and if he can put you in a place where your weakness prevails, and then he can work a work on you to cause you to fall. His objective is to make you want what is not morally right for you to have.

Think about Eve. Wanting to be more like God wasn't a bad thing. That's what we all should be striving for on a daily basis. In fact, what Eve didn't know was that they were more like God than they knew. They were made in His likeness and image. What was even more important than being like God was the fact that God was truly with them. Her need should have been for restraint, obedience, and contentment. The want--- to have more knowledge wasn't a want at all. In their obedience, they would have gained all the knowledge man needed and that was to know that God loves them. They truly had the greatest knowledge of all. Once you know that God loves you, it far outweighs any information you could ever obtain. All I'm saying to you is all that you need, God has already provided!

Wanting a husband is not a bad thing; you must remember that God has the provisions to cause you to be found. Instead of allowing Satan to beguile you into believing that someone else's husband is yours, why don't you rely on the fact that God will present you with what you need when it's time? God will do it and it won't be through trickery, deceit, forgery, or sin. I'm simply saying that there's nothing wrong with you wanting a man but it is wrong when you take Satan up on his advances to help you find a man. You don't need the enemy to help you find anything; especially something (a husband) that you aren't supposed to be looking for. You will be found (if that's what you desire) and it will work because God will be in the plan.

The whole objective of the enemy is to invade you. His desire is to make you see that if you want it, you can have it. When Satan devised a plan to tempt God it was based on if you do, then I'll do. Each time Jesus gave him a definite response that he could not tempt the Lord thy God. Satan couldn't give Jesus anything because everything already belonged to Him. See that's exactly what God wants us to know!!! If everything already belongs to your Father, all you have to do is ask and wait.

Satan was crazy enough to offer someone something who owned it all. Satan doesn't have the authority to give you anything or to take anything from you, except that God allows. He (Satan) only presents opportunity for worldly possessions to entice and create lustful beings. Isn't it good to know that what God has for you it's yours? So knowing this, you must stand firm like Christ did against the enemy and realize that no matter how you feel, you refuse to be tempted.

Watch Out For Those Seeds

When you allow the seed to become planted, you're invaded but unless a seed is nurtured, it won't grow. You my sister have the authority to cast down everything that exalts itself above and against the knowledge of God. When the planted seed of lust tries to tell you that if you do it, you can repent, you cut that booger down. How? By saying out loud, "Satan you cannot tempt God's Daughter!" When the thought of impurity first presents itself, it is your responsibility to cut it down. The seed can't produce fruit if it is uprooted. As soon as I think something that I know isn't of God, I declare, "Satan you cannot plant no seeds in the garden of my mind!" He doesn't have the authority to invade not even my thoughts. This is called taking authority over what God has given you...a sound mind.

Sin starts with the eyes. You see something or someone that looks good to you and instead of moving on, the photogenic seed that has been planted with your eyes, stores the image in your memory. You find yourself replaying the scene over and over again. Each time, your body is beginning to react according to what your eyes have seen. Your mind is now entangled by what your eyes have seen and you began to secretly crave. Cravings are explosive! Think about a pregnant woman craving something or even a drug addict. If you keep craving something hard and long enough, you'll eventually grab it.

Once those demons are fully aware that you are storing what you saw, the next step is to operate on your ears. Your ears are an important part of your body. Think about it. We believe not because of what we saw, but because of what we've heard. Yes, my belief in Jesus Christ didn't come because I saw Him on Calvary but because I heard the story of his being there and after having heard it so many times, I eventually began to believe it. You and no one else can convince me that my Savior did not die on a cross on Calvary's hill. So as you see, if you hear something enough, you'll eventually begin to believe it. That's why demons always have a way of bringing other folks with demons around you. This is so that they can feed your ears. It slowly begins to reach every part of you. It's a sure fire infestation and a complete infiltration.

With me, all a man had to do was say he went to church or loved God. My demons were connected to whoremongering men who were well dressed and well versed. It was my belief that if a man could take care of God's business, he could take care of me. This all stemmed from a seed that was planted when I was a teenager. Although I'd made a pack to never mess with my pastor, yours was not untouchable. I later pleaded with God to take this away from me. I just didn't want to be his mistress and the fact that he was God's man was double jeopardy for me.

Seeds grow when you nourish them and so do sin. When nourished, craved sin becomes committed sin and we know that accomplished sin opens the door for not just physical death but even worse, spiritual death. I know you're wondering well what if the seed was planted and I didn't have the spiritual knowledge to cut it down? Find your pastor or any spiritual person who walks in the will of God. They'll have enough faith to usher you into prayer. If not, you'll find yourself in intentional sins committed because you know the truth but want to do according to your flesh. What if it was a seed that was sown when I saw my mother or my aunts cheat? What if I saw a couple in the church sleep around when I was young? It very well could be learned behavior that causes you to desire another person's mate. The eyes is the gateway for many things because it is with our eyes that we gain instructions how to. Whether we learn good things or bad things, our eyes are the gateway to learning. This is why it is so important that we become examples of the truth because we never know who is watching us.

Chapter Two
The Little Girl Who's Watching

Sharmen

Sharmen was about eight years old when her mother warned her that what went on in her house, stayed in her house. She didn't quite understand the seriousness of the quote until she noticed the belt firmly wrapped around her mother's hand. As she braced herself for the whooping, she went over and over in her mind, replaying the words her mother had just said. Sharmen after a couple of licks and a blistered butt realized that her mother must have been upset with her for telling grandma that Mr. Sparks visited them and brought ice-cream and food.

Sharmen had no idea that grandma wasn't supposed to know, but judging by the whooping, it was top secret and she'd never tell anyone else. Mr. Sparks was a nice man who was a deacon at their church. He always brought Sharmen something good when he came to visit and because of this, she was so excited when she saw his big shinny car turn the corner. Even mother was excited to see him. After mom and Mr. Sparks put her to bed, they'd go in mother's room and close the door. She never knew what time Mr. Sparks would leave but he was certain to be gone by morning.

At church, Mr. Sparks rarely spoke to Sharmen's mom but he always made sure to give Sharmen a great big hug. By the time she was twelve, she became aware that Mr. Sparks had his very own family. That didn't stop him from coming over frequently and mostly at night. Sometimes in the daytime he would come in his work uniform but that would only be to drop off money for bills, or food for them.

PROVERBS 22:6

"Train up a child in the way he shall go and when he is old he will not depart from it."

A lot of children are witnesses to forbidden relationships at early ages. A child never views their mother's choices as wrong or sinful but with age, secrets are revealed. Often the child never thinks it's a bad relationship because the person came baring good gifts. The gift often places a shadow over the fact that it's the wrong type of relationship. So the child grows up with the misconceived illusion that it's okay to be the girlfriend of a married man as long as he: pays the bills, buys groceries, gives the kids money, and make everyone happy.

No doubt, the child who is now a grown woman has a warped sense of thinking concerning married men. It doesn't matter that they hear the preacher say that it's wrong; the fact is that if he hadn't been in her life, things would not have been easy. So because there has been no known penalty for the sin that has been committed, the child (now an adult) thinks that it must have been okay. Children see things through the eyes of innocence and often their fragile minds don't grasp the reality of what is right.

Learned Behavior

Learned behavior is normally formulated by what is seen and it incorporates visual as factual and thus become appropriate to the one who has witnessed it. It's knowledgeable behavior that we've acquired through informal training of what we've seen and it becomes instinctual. That's why I believe that when a girl sees her mother as a mistress, she in turn will not prevent herself from taking the same route. Even though it had all the evidence of something wrong, it must have been right because mom did it. It is so hard for children to separate what they saw growing up- from their lives, when they become adults. This separation only comes about when the person makes a conscience choice to separate themselves from the sins of their parents. For some, it becomes a generational curse in which they fail to fight to become free from it.

What you do as a mother affects your children tremendously. Not just your daughters are affected but so are your sons. Take a young man who watched his mother cheat on every man she was with. If his own mother, who he loves more than anyone is a whore-monger, then you aren't exempt. So the reality is that he'll treat someone's daughter as if she's cheap, or a liar because he saw these traits in the woman he loved the most. We must realize that our children are watching us and whether we train them in disobedience or obedience to the Word of God, the training is still there.

What is even more detrimental to a child is when we are practicing religion that says what we should and should not do? To a child it becomes significant that if the adult doesn't respect or honor God enough to obey Him, why should he even believe that there is a God. For some reason the world has it set that only children obey. That is exactly why kids say, "I can't wait until I get old and I don't have to obey." I tell my kids that it's easier to obey me rather than God and once you stop obeying me, then it's time for you to start completely obeying God. I am here to help you transition from obeying me to obeying God. God's rules are much more important than mine.

The same lessons in obedience that we impart to our children are mere guidelines to those, which are imparted on us by God through His Word. Now then, how is it you propose to bring up a child in the way of obedience and you yourself can't seem to find the faith to obey?

My heart bleeds for children who grow up never seeing the value of obedience. Especially since the world's consequences for disobedience are not always fair. Therefore why subject your child to becoming a part of an unfair system all because you never taught them by example. Do as I say and not as I do, doesn't work anymore. It's a trick of the enemy to make children think that it's okay to sin or do what's wrong when you grow up.

The Church Is Not A Place for Sin

What makes the church the largest joke around is that church folks are building new buildings, and in these buildings, folks are doing more sinning against the body than in the club.

Everybody confessing salvation but no one is living saved. Although the church is indeed a hospital for those who practiced sin but have come to the realization that they need the Word of God to set restraints, restore, rebuild, rebuke, and reconstruct their lives; it has also been a breeding ground for sin. The church is not a place for immoral behavior, and I am so tired of people using a place where games should never been played as a playground. The church is a holy place and it is not a pick up spot!

We had an upstairs room in our church when I was young and the kids were having more sex in the church than you could ever imagine. There was nothing sacred about the Lord's house to the teens because what they'd witnessed. It was already tainted with adults who were saturated in sexual sins. Believe me, whether you want to or not, your actions train children.

Now when I look back, I see only a few of us that were determined to stay with God after getting older and finding new meaning to Christianity and the church. My heart hurts for those who couldn't escape the grasp of learned behaviors and are in church doing just what they saw done when we were young. I know people have been instructed to go to church if you want to be found by a good man, but the church is not a pick up spot. You actually take the church to the sacred building, to forsake not the assembling of saints together to gain encouragement from one another, to gain spiritual relationships, but not to create immoral relationships.

EPHESIANS 5:3

"But fornication and all uncleanness or covetousness, let it not even be named among you, as is fitting for saints." (KJV)

"But among you there must not be even a hint of sexual immorality or of any kind of impurity, or of greed, because these are improper for God's holy people." (NIV)

The Holy Cop Out

The church is to be separate from the world, and the building ought to be a place where a child can learn to do what is right (by watching HOLY people). Even when their homes are festered with sin, they ought to see something totally different in the church. Yeah, don't forget the holy cop out... "We all have sinned and come short of the glory of God." We use this scripture to validate our intentional sin and to demonstrate the fact that we all are going to sin and God should expect it from us; thus, making the scripture our cop out for sinful activities. It is simply pride (lusts' brother) that gives us the authority to do us and our stupidity that causes us to believe that God is going to give us the opportunity to repent. Some folks would even have you believe that all you have to do is believe and then you can live any way you like. I do believe that many will be saying, "Lord, but didn't I." And He's going to say, "Depart from me you worker of iniquity."

MATTHEW 7:21-23

21"Not every one that saith unto me, Lord, Lord, shall enter into the kingdom of heaven; but he that doeth the will of my Father which is in heaven. 22Many will say to me in that day, Lord, Lord, have we not prophesied in thy name? and in thy name have cast out devils? and in thy name done many wonderful works? 23And then will I profess unto them, I never knew you: depart from me, ye that work iniquity."

The Good Example

I do believe that for us to believe that we can live any way because that's how we want to, is ignorant. We are going to be held accountable for every deed done in our flesh. We will also be held accountable for those whom we've misguided or even misled. There is always a child somewhere who is watching you. That's why it is so important that you be a good example. I also believe that there is a line between who our kids should watch and we should be directing. By this I mean, we shouldn't teach our kids to watch celebrities unless we know that they are saved. We are responsible for being the purest example of obedience, righteousness, love, holiness, and all the other fruits of the spirit, before our children. As saints of God, we become responsible for not only our children, but the children of others. When we neglect to become the good example, we often destroy a child's ability to trust and believe. I'll always remember when the example of all I wanted to be in a woman, turned into the woman I dreaded becoming but became. She wasn't a good example and when I found this out, it crushed me.

CHAPTER THREE
I Shall Never Forget

I'll never forget the emotions I felt as a teenager when I found out that a woman whom I'd admired in the church was the mistress of a pastor. She'd been with this man for years and he'd made sure that she was taken care of.

One part of me couldn't believe that a woman as pretty as she was, who had it going on like she did, would settle for being second. I was shamed for her and I felt so much pity for her. She showed me a diamond ring that he bought her and I was amazed. Then the feelings of shame and pity disappeared and were replaced with feelings of approval because at least she wasn't going without.

To me, she became a true liability to man she loved and he became her financial bank. He was obligated to take care of her and she was obligated to satisfy his lust. What did I learn? I learned as long as he was taking care of things, it didn't matter who he was or who he had. My life changed because of this, I believe.

Be Careful What You Say To A Teenage Girl, It Could Shape Her Life!

As I look back, I realize that she wasn't my only influence. My daddy in one of his drunken moments said, "A woman should never be broke if she has a vagina." He added, "If a man is looking up in your face and breathing your air, he ought to be doing something for you." "You shouldn't have to ask a man for anything but just in case he isn't a real man and he doesn't offer, you need to tell him what you want and need." His statements became just as important to me as my name. As you see, I obtained two of the most horrible lessons I'd ever learn, as a teenage girl.

I had safely trusted in the image of a woman who I thought was totally wrapped up in God, and found that her outside life didn't equal to the life she portrayed in the church. And I listened intently to a drunk that was giving his daughter wisdom in order to keep her from getting used.

It's like the enemy has tapped into your future, and he knows exactly what it will take to push you off course. God had placed a godly role model right before me in my grandmother (The late L.B. Ford). She was exactly like the woman I chose and she wore the finest of clothes, she had her own business, and she was beautiful. Yet the enemy put someone a little flashier before me so I would desire to be like her. That's why we have to be careful and mindful of the little girl and teenage girls who are watching us.

The Outside Doesn't Determine The Inside

I watch how my sixteen year old is in awe with women who dress really nice. She has an eye for fashion and if you can dress, then she likes you. I have begun to teach her that just because a person appears to have it going on outwardly it doesn't mean that they're fixed up on the inside. I teach her that outward adornment doesn't hold any weight against the heart of a righteous woman. The righteous have it going on inside, and on the outside. Just like my grandmother, she was a woman of integrity by every mean. I teach her this so that she won't get caught up in the perception of the eyes. To me, she is the little girl who's watching and it is my responsibility to live holy before her, and to teach her what is right. Now, just because I'm teaching my girls what is right doesn't mean that they won't see someone doing wrong. I pray that my influence on them will cause them to recognize the enemy for who he is.

So now as the church saturates in the dispensation of the Holy Spirit, it is my prayer that young girls see women who not only praise and worship God, but women who wait on God. I believe in the case of the woman I admired, it was the misfortune of her deciding to be God in her own life. I know that if she would have waited on God, she would have been some gentleman's loving wife instead of His Mistress.

1 TIMOTHY 4:12

Let no man despise thy youth; but be thou an example of the believers, in word, in conversation, in charity, in spirit, in faith, in purity.

TITUS 2:3-5

3The aged women likewise, that they be in behaviour as becometh holiness, not false accusers, not given to much wine, teachers of good things; 4That they may teach the young women to be sober, to love their husbands, to love their children, 5To be discreet, chaste, keepers at home, good, obedient to their own husbands, that the word of God be not blasphemed.

Chapter Four

When Lust Prevails

Sharmen

Sharmen decided that today she was going to work late due to a large caseload that Mandery had neglected to take care of because of lack of time. He'd become so pre-occupied with marital problems until he'd allowed some of his most important clients to slip through his fingers. She was determined to do whatever she could to insure that they wouldn't lose any more customers; even if it meant she had to stay all night. When Walter the night janitor announced that he would be leaving for the night, she waved goodbye and as soon as he disappeared in the elevator, she pulled off her jacket. Her shirt with the lace bow in the front was too provocative for Walter and she wasn't going to be the reason he had a heart attack. After she chuckled because of her thoughts, she pulled off her jet-black stockings.

Sharmen walked into Mandery's office to retrieve the stack of files off his desk. She gathered as many folders as she could and took them to the office adjacent to his. After she cleared a spot on the desk to work, she couldn't help but think of how happy Mandery would be that she'd completed all the files. With everything he was going through at home, the least she could do was make him happy.

The Method of The Enemy's Madness

Understand me when I say that the enemy is always on target concerning his prey. He knows your weakness and he knows what you want at any given moment; especially when your want is based on lust, greed, sex, and not out of necessity. There is a method called set-up and wait. The enemy will coast you into set-up position, and he's patient enough to keep the demons taunting until you fall. We allow the lust to prevail in our lives when we have characteristics that are not of God.

Don't Become a Busy Body

The story before describes a busy-body in action. He owned the firm and if he didn't tell her to mess with the files on his desk, she shouldn't have messed with them. Women find all kinds of situations to get in because they're too busy minding other folks business, instead of focusing on their souls. This even applies to the woman who might be working for a man but doesn't have ulterior motives. Sometimes as a woman we get too overly helpful.

There's nothing wrong with helping a man who has asked for your help, but when you do things that you aren't asked to do (especially in someone's personal space), this could speak language that you don't want spoken. Most women skilled in getting the man will tell you that they have mastered the find-something-to-do-trait. This trait in tells cleaning his house while he's gone, making his surroundings comfortable, or even cooking a meal for him if you stay over.

Women learn early that if you do something for someone, you gain their affection but this is not always true. You could easily give your all and do all you can for someone and if a person doesn't want you, nothing you do is going to make them want you and then you've wasted your time. Use your time wisely and remember that any free time you have is soul fixing time. This is time for you to build on the relationship with God that you've started. He's the only one that if you can be busy in well doing, not only will appreciate you for it, but will be reward for it.

Mandery & Christine

Mandery and Christine moved into their bedroom to discuss the latest episode in their marriage. He'd come home to find his sofa on the porch and a brand new sofa in the living room. Christine asked him to buy a new sofa and he'd distinctively told her no. He was furious to see that she'd disregarded his direct request not to buy another sofa. For Mandery, this was the last straw. After a heated discussion between the two of them, it was apparent that Christine wasn't going to explain why she did what she did. Mandery packed himself an overnight bag and slammed the door behind him. He refused to sleep under the same roof with a woman who would deliberately disobey him.

A Candidate For Sin

As you have life, the enemy will constantly try to catch you in a trap, and if you don't recognize when your life is being interfered with by the enemy, you'll fail every time. Satan knows when you are an able candidate to fall into sin. I'll never forget the day I met the man who I deemed worthy of having me as his mistress. I was in class one night and in walks this well dressed, chocolate, handsome, arrogant man who smelled better than any man I'd ever smelt before. He was very well spoken and then he voiced his opinion that wasn't only egotistic, but very chauvinistic. BING! There it was. The bait that Satan put on the string to entrap me. My ego was big enough to make him eat his words.

Self or Selfish Pride

Instead of me recognizing the trick of the enemy, I was ready to play trick or treat. Selfish-pride is our worst enemy. There's a difference between selfish-pride and selfless-pride. Here's my definition of the two.

Selfless-pride is when you pride yourself on the fact that you belong to God, and you make sure that your representation of Him is a sure reflection of who He is. It is the ability for others to perceive who you are, and with whom you belong too, by how you act. You have a proper sense of your own self value. Instead of a feeling of superiority, it's a satisfied feeling in how God has created you ("fearfully and wonderfully" refer to Psalms 139:14) and having pleasure in the process of you becoming what He intends on you to become.

Selfish-pride is when you take on the spirit of superiority as part of yourself, and go out of your way to make sure that everything is about you. With this pride your motto becomes, me-my-and-I, and everything in between doesn't concern you. You have an improper sense of your own self-value. When lust prevails, it gets you in a place where selfish-pride means you are only concerned about what makes you happy, or what will make your life easier.

Sharmen

Sharmen had been busy working for well over two hours. The office was tranquil and because she was alone, she decided to get too comfortable. She slipped off her blouse and work in her lace Victoria Secret bra that was revealing all her secrets. She laughed at the thought of Mandery coming back to the office and catching her in her bra, but quickly pushed the fantasy out of her mind. There was no need in fantasizing about a man who wasn't ready to play the games that she was ready to play. Then, for a quick second she thought about how her mother had been a man's mistress all of her life. She without hesitation pushed that thought completely away and decided that any man was better than no man at all.

So often in life lust prevails by making us believe that we had better accept what was handed to us. It is the power of persuasion of lust that depreciates our true value. We begin to think less of ourselves because of what we don't have, than to expect more because of what God has already given us. It's almost like going into a basketball game already accepting defeat even though the game hasn't even started. When we make up our minds to entertain what is less than appropriate, and make up our minds to follow through on our thoughts, lust prevails.

Mandery

When Mandery pulled into the parking lot, he noticed Sharmen's little red convertible Lexus in the same spot it was in when he'd left the office. He quickly descended from his Bentley and jogged to the entrance of the building. He put his security code in, opened the door, and walked over to the security desk to check the daily log. Walter had signed out two hours ago and had left a note on his board that he'd left Ms. Sharmen, at her request, working late. He didn't want to startle her but he was curious about what she was working on.

He'd given her the files that he'd needed her to work on earlier and thought she should have already completed them by now. Mandery decided to take the stairs instead of the elevator and as soon as he stepped off, he noticed the light in the office across from his.

To his surprise, there she was in a black laced bra. The vision was breath taking as her curly black hair flowed down past her shoulders. He'd never seen her hair down because she'd always kept it pinned up. She was beautiful and although he'd already known it, it was more apparent now than usual.

Sharmen & Mandery

Sharmen felt an uneasy feeling over take her. She felt as if someone was watching her so she slowly lifted her head to see if there were anything to the eerie feeling she'd began to feel.

She jumped. There he was the man she'd fantasized about for months and there she was revealing to him the secrets of her body that she'd always wanted him to see.

"Sharmen I didn't mean to scare you. I see I'm interrupting so I'll just go to my office."

Mandery didn't want to seem like a boy who'd never seen breast before. His body was reacting and he seemed to have no self-control.

Sharmen put on her blouse and then her jacket. There was absolutely no way that she was going through the trouble of putting her stockings back on. After she was presentable, she went to his office to explain. She could clearly see that he'd gotten enough of an eyeful of her beautiful breasts to be alarmed. Mandery adjusted his pants and quickly sat down behind his desk.

"Is everything okay Mr. Jacobs?

"Sharmen I've told you over and over again to call me Mandery. If you think me spending the night at my office is okay, then everything is fine."

"I really don't know how to respond to that so I think I better just leave."

"Sharmen, you don't have to leave, in fact I could use the company." He said trying to muster up a smile through a lustful stare.

"I think it would be best because..." And before she could say another word, their lips were locked so tight

until it would have taken a crow bar to pry them apart.

A small voice told Mandery not to do it but an over powering voice said, "What the heck! She wants you too." Mandery decided the need to listen to the voice that was ushering him towards fleshy benefits. He'd never felt more disrespected by Christine than he did right now and he was going to prove to himself that he wasn't a weak man. Time and time again, he'd seen nice men being taken advantage of by women. They always took kindness as a weakness.

Just as he was about to rub his hands under her skirt, feeling the texture of her long smooth legs, his phone rang. He had no intentions on answering it but he'd forgotten about his office technology. Because of the modern technology, he'd purchased, whenever he failed to answer his phone, if the person calling left a message you could hear it through surrounding speakers in his office. It was Christine. She was explaining that he needed to come home so she could explain to him about the sofa. He slowly released Sharmen but couldn't resist pecking her on the lips once more.

You Can Escape Temptation

There is no temptation known to man under the sun that an escape hasn't already been planned and provided.

---

1 CORINTHIANS 10:13

"There hath no temptation taken you but such as is common to man: but God is faithful, who will not suffer you to be tempted above that ye are able; but will with the temptation also make a way to escape, that ye may be able to bear it."

You have a distinct opportunity to get out of anything that you are not supposed to be in. I can remember how right before I was getting ready to sin against my body, my phone would rang. What would have been the perfect excuse for escape for me, was to say, "I need to handle this phone call."

With me, God would even go through other

measures. I can't count how many times I was getting ready to sin, and the guy wouldn't get ready. Yeah! Of course he was ashamed but I knew it was God's perfect escape for me.

Sometimes, we'd get so caught up in what our flesh desired until we ignored the escape. I know I'm not the only one who's been there. I've been on my way to a rendezvous and my car just stops. God is precise concerning his children, and you must know that it's just not sex that He'll send an escape for. He'll provide an escape whenever you are getting into a position to sin against God.

Praise Break Time!!! Thank you Lord for the escape.

A Missed Opportunity

Nevertheless, people often overlook the escape. They are so caught up in the right now of sin, until their minds are clouded by the expectations of what is going to be. Then what is the strangest thing to me is that after the situation is over we start wishing that we wouldn't have fallen into it. I would jump in the tub like I could erase what I'd just done. Although I could clean my body, the soap didn't have the power to clean my soul, my mind, and my heart.

What is even crazier is that the same enemy who persuades you to allow lust to prevail, he's the same one who tries to overload you with guilt and shame. He'll say things like:

- You know God doesn't love fornicators and adulterers.

- You are too dirty to go to that church; and your hands aren't holy enough to lift up holy hands.

- You got to be kidding if you think the church folks aren't going to know that you've been sinning all night long.

- You need to just stay away from the church until you get clean.

Sin Is Shameful

The same sucker, who used his demonic friends to suck you up in the trenches of sin, is the same one who smashes guilt and shame in your face like a cream pie. In case you didn't know, demons talk loud and clear. Especially, when they are trying to demean you, destroy your worth, cast down God's love for you, and separate you from God.

See, if sin was okay, then it wouldn't be so shameful. I notice how people who have decided to live in sin, (because they feel this is how they were created) react. They often watch curiously to see who's looking at them. It's almost like they just know you're going to watch them, and some begin to act out by becoming loud. It's like they say, "You aren't going to look at me because you see my sin as shameful, I'm going to give you another reason to look at me, and it will be because I'm loud. Either way, whether we choose a life of sin or sin privately, we tend to be ashamed of it.

Don't Hide From Me Because You Can't Hide From God

I have never understood why we'll allow lust to prevail in our lives and then be ashamed of it before man. Get this, we do it before an all knowing God who has a heaven or hell to put us in, and we'll hide from folks who can't do anything but talk. We have such a warped sense of thinking when it comes to sin. We would rather people approve of us or perceive us as good when in fact, our good doesn't mean anything to Christ. When we decide to allow sin to prevail, we had better be able to deal with the consequences of our sins. We need to become more aware of lust trying to prevail in our lives.

What you see isn't always what you get! My grandmother use to say, "The grass isn't always greener on the other side." Lust has a way of causing us to block out the reality of the situation. It has a way of causing us to want what we should not have just because it looks good.

Don't Let Your Eyes Overload Your

Have you ever just eaten dinner and a Red Lobster commercial come on? Those lobsters and shrimps look so good until you want to go out and buy some. You forget all about the chicken you just finished. We never question the fact that if you do go to Red Lobster, you are going to have to pay for that meal that you won't eat because you really weren't hungry.

Why? When things look good, we rarely consider what could be wrong with them. The same with relationships, lust makes things look so good until we never look for the bad. He looks good, but I wonder how many women does he have? He drives a nice car; I wonder does he sell drugs to ride in it? He has the finest body; I wonder does he share it with men and women? See, we need to search out the full situation. We allow lust to cause us to be ignorant to facts.

I worked for a loan company and have been in finance for a while now. I just can't get your paycheck stub and approve you for a loan on the basis that you make money. I have to get all up in your business to see not only if you make enough money, but if you can afford to take on something else on top of what you already have. I even have to find out whether or not you've been worthy of paying back what you already owe someone else. So, if I have to do all of this to approve you for a loan, why don't you do all this to approve someone in your life and your bed? Because of lust, we give away our most prized possessions. We never think about the aftermath of our decision until we are put in a place where we can't help but deal with our choice.

You Better Be Careful

What happens you allow lust to prevail, and you give your body to someone who has AIDS or another sexually transmitted disease? What happens if you get pregnant? What quality of life would your child have as the seed of a married man? What happens to you emotionally when he promises to deliver and can't? How does God feel about me right now? How do I feel about God? We should ask these questions before we allow lust to prevail.

I know you are wondering, how do I keep lust from prevailing in my life? Give no ear to the devil. As soon as you see the enemy trying to get in God's business, you snatch him down. Any and everything that has to do with you is God's business because you belong to God. The enemy has no place showing you anything, enticing you with anything, or offering you anything or should I say, "ANYONE." If nothing you are being offered agrees with your spirit, then it is not of God.

If You Got A Little Money

Here's another number one factor why lust prevails...MONEY! The Bible says that "the love of money is the root of all evil." The love of money will cause you to sell your most prized possession and give your most valuable gift to a man. You have to make sure that you know who your provider is. If you know that God is your provider, then you won't get ensnared in a forbidden lustful relationship. God has given you one thing on earth to manage and that is your body. Some of us are pleading for God to give us other things and He's saying, "You're not managing the most valuable thing I've already given you!" We must refuse to abuse our bodies for the sake of having money. Don't allow lust to prevail in your life. Keep the below scriptures in your heart.

---

1 CORINTHIANS 10:13 (NIV)

"No temptation has seized you except what is common to man. And God is faithful; he will not let you be tempted beyond what you can bear. But when you are tempted, he will also provide a way out so that you can stand up under it."

1 THESSALONIANS 4:3-5

3"For this is the will of God, your sanctification: that you should abstain from sexual immorality; 4that each of you should know how to possess his own vessel in sanctification and honor, 5not in passion of lust, like the Gentiles who do not know God;"

Chapter Five

His Mistress

I have known women who have lived and died, and the only thing that they are now remembered for is having been some man's mistress. Who is she? His mistress is the woman who has chosen to live her life as the second fiddle in a man's life. The object of her affection isn't the man she's decided to contaminate her spirit with, but simply herself.

She's made a vow to make herself happy no matter whom she hurts in the process. I can hear some woman screaming that's not me! My sister, yes, it is you. See, I speak from experience because I was his mistress. I wasn't concerned about anyone except for Danyelle.

Who Is She?

His mistress is not always looking for love, but instead affirmation that she is fulfilling an inner emptiness that she's been longing for. She's the single parent who's been praying for God to send her a spouse. She's the vulnerable woman who believes that she's finally being validated as a woman. She's sometimes even the one with innocent intentions who doesn't know how to say, "No." What I'm trying to get you to see is that she's a woman with many faces, in different situations.

It makes me laugh when I see how women in the church treat some women. It's like they target or label the woman who tries to look nice or is their perception of a whoremonger or a mistress. I say to you that this is the main reason why women are able to operate as a mistress. Women are too busy looking and targeting the wrong type of woman. A true mistress is just as concerned about her reputation as the next person. Because she's operating under the unction and persuasion of a lustful, secretive spirit, you'll never know who she is unless she tells you. Why? She's not out to hurt you, she's only out to make life easier for herself. Get this...sometimes she don't even want your man. Your man gets caught up in the equation because he's an easy, giving prey. She's decided to become a mistress in a lot of cases because it's easier.

Trust me; no one wants the reputation of breaking up a happy home. Even if the home wasn't happy, who do you think people will blame? Often, she doesn't want the stigma or responsibility; she just wants some of the benefits of your home. When you find a mistress who wants to become a wife, she's in search for something just like the man is. Most of the time it's the power or prestige that comes with being the wife of the man who she's secretly with. Trust me, I don't care how much a man thinks he wasn't a target, if a mistress ends up married to the man she was cheating with, she wasn't his target...he was hers.

All About The Benjamin Baby

Take me for example, I was newly divorced and had dated a couple of single guys who were all about themselves. When Mr. Married presented me with a couple of wonderful trips, I wasn't concerned about breaking up his home. I was only concerned about him sharing the wealth of his home. See, a real mistress is only concerned about the handouts that your husband is willing to give. She doesn't care that your money is his money; all she's concerned with is that the money finds its way into her hands. If she's not in search for money, it's sex.

This takes me back to the spirit of lust. If you find a mistress who declares in her heart that she is the wife, you find a woman who has allowed lust to camouflage itself as love. Lust can transcend into all types of emotions. It's just like a lizard. A lizard changes its' color and blends in with the environment around him; so does lust. When lust changes to love, the mistress has begun to safely trust in your husband. He becomes a god in her life. Love-lust makes her believe that he's supposed to be in her life, and that they would have a better life than the life he has with you. This is when the mistress becomes a problem.

With all her heart, she'll begin to believe that it is her place to be beside your husband. It is at this point that she'll have the audacity to sit in the same place as you; even in the same church as you. This is when she can become deadly!!!

Don't Lay Out the Welcome Mat for Demons

Remember, demons are working in the situation even from the beginning. The longer they stay around, the stronger they get. The more she becomes guided by emotions rather than by the spirit of God. When lust and his brothers take over the house of your emotions (your soul), you'll do anything. It is vitally important that men realize that they are threading on dangerous territory, when they get caught up in a relationship with a woman who is willing to be a mistress. The same applies to a man who is willing to allow you to be his mistress. When spirits gain strength, it's hard to break them down. They were built upon what they want, and if you try to interfere with what they want, they will break you down.

I need women to understand that there is nothing light about being a mistress. There is nothing real about a relationship that is not founded upon the Word of God. And if it is not founded or ordained by God, then it is set up by the devil. Anything that the devil sets up can and will become deadly. I get so appalled when I hear that a wife is intentionally trying to find her husband's mistress. Matter of fact, here's a word to a wise wife…stop trying to seek out your husband's mistress and pray for him and her. You do not have to go looking for the enemy. And mistress, know that the devil is in operation but he's not just in you, he's in the man who has decided that he needed you as well.

God has allowed me to expose my own life and not to be ashamed so that you can be delivered. I was so caught up in someone else's life, until I forgot about my own life. Love-lust entangled me and when the chips fell, I realized that I was so caught up. I was so blinded by the haze. It's like being caught on the highway in fog. You become almost like a zombie. In fact, you are just like a wife in another house. It starts off as an independent type relationship and the next thing you know, he's putting demands on you that he can't even put on his wife. Then you start shutting out the outside world, because he's too afraid that the wrong voice with the right message- might speak life, and you'll awaken from the trance of the enemy. He's afraid that you'll begin to see through the fog.

Don't Be A Pawn

You become so weak to the advances of the enemy that prayer lines stop helping. Matters of fact, most mistresses don't even go to church unless that's where the man is and she hates sermons about adultery. Most Pastors who dip in the sin of adultery don't even preach on the subject, and this is the pastor she searches out. The objective of the enemy is to get you so far away from God until he's in full control of your life.

Don't you dare put this book down!!!

I am declaring you free and free this day. "He whom the Son hath set free is free indeed." In Jesus name and by faith I call it done. The enemy wants to use you as a pawn to destroy the family. It is his desire to eliminate anything on earth that represents the relationship that God desires with His children. If he can get you to stand in agreement with lust of the eyes, lust of the flesh, and the pride of life, then he can destroy not just the lives of the marriage he's targeting, but your life as well.

Don't you know that the enemy never uses anyone he doesn't intend on destroying as well? He's just that dirty. He'll even have you so caught up until you'll pray to a righteous God to make this man yours. It even sounds crazy reading that we will go to God to bless us in our mess, doesn't it? Imagine how much pity God has for you, as His very own child, asking Him to defile everything that He stands for in order for you to have some earthly pleasure.

My God this day, change our hearts!!!

In case you didn't know, God will not honor a prayer that goes against His word. This is a prayer that is amidst. You can't keep playing with God like this and He won't keep playing with you. This book is some of you all's last warning. God has been urging me to write this book. I wrote and finished it but the enemy was making things so crazy around me, until I prolonged getting it into yours hands.

Your deliverance is riding on my life (literally), because if my disobedience causes your delayed deliverance, God will charge me. And after I have given you this to you and you fail to listen, you are no longer required on me.

MARK 6:11

"And whosoever shall not receive you, nor hear you, when ye depart thence, shake off the dust under your feet for a testimony against them. Verily I say unto you,

It shall be more tolerable for Sodom and Gomorrha in the day of judgment, than for that city."

If I don't put it out there for you to see, I will be held accountable. Why he chose me? Because I know how you feel. I know how it feels to be praying every day for God to send me a husband but to no avail. I know how it feels to see friends with husbands that they are cheating on, and all I wanted was a piece of husband. I know how it seems to feel lonely at night, when you pull down the covers and turn off the lights. I also know how Satan will manipulate you into giving yourself to a man that is not yours. So, who better to write this book than me?

His mistress, it is not my objective to beat you over the head. I just want the words that I am writing to penetrate your heart. You'll be so surprised to know that if you get the man, he'll not be the man you thought you were getting. You'll find out that you really should have left him where he was. I personally know women who have gotten the men and are going through the same thing, or even worse things, than they put their former wives through. You reap what you sow! Another factor is, as soon as you get him, you have to deal with the demons of trust. The lack of trust is enough to drive you absolutely crazy. You'll be up in the middle of the night going through business cards, pockets, and cell phones.

Nothing in this life just happens. If a man wasn't with the woman he was supposed to be with, God would not have allowed it to happen. Even our very own will is no match for God's Will for our lives. Whether by permission or permissive will, it is who he married. No, we don't always wait on God to find our spouses. Nevertheless, when we get married, God holds us to the sanction of our choices. Have you ever wondered why it is so hard for him to leave his wife?

Christine

Christine honored her God and her husband but lately it seemed that her husband didn't appreciate her. She'd help him build their advertising agency from the ground up and after the birth of their daughter; he'd insisted that she stayed home. At first it was okay staying at home not getting a paycheck because Mandery wasn't monitoring her spending. Now all of a sudden he was trying to control every penny she spent.

When he married her, she had just graduated from college and was working two jobs. Even though she liked nice things, her mother had always taught her that she should buy nice things and give them to people who needed them the most. Since she'd been in high school, she'd bought Dooney purses and other named brand things and gave them to the women at the shelter she visited twice a week. Her mother had taught her the value in giving.

She couldn't understand why Mandery had started trying to keep up with every penny she spent and she had never felt it necessary to tell anyone what she did for the shelter. Her Bible told her that if you did something for someone, you weren't supposed to tell anyone. She'd never thought that it was keeping secrets from her husband, because she really didn't think it mattered. But now, she had no choice but to tell him. She'd known he said not to buy a new couch so she went *to the local Thrift Shop and purchased a used sofa for them. She brought it home, cleaned it up, and even to her it looked new. She knew that it past the test of looking new to others because Mandery had a fit when he came home. He'd never stayed away from home and she wasn't certain if tonight would be his first night. All she could do was pray that the Lord would bring him home so she could explain.*

Marriage Is Not A Joke

Marriage is not a joke and although easy to get in, it's hard to get out of. There is no doubt in my mind that thousands of people are married to one another for the wrong reasons. God will allow us to do things and then transform the very action we took without Him into the very best thing we've ever done. That's why you can't go by a half told story of a broken home or a neglected spouse. Most of the times when people start affairs, they start on a whim of what the other spouse is not doing or is doing that isn't to their liking; that's still no reason to have an affair. Marriage takes communicating to the one you're married to. What good does it do you to tell an outsider about what your spouse isn't doing? What good is it doing you to allow a married person (to use you as a human garbage can), to dump their problems on you? If their spouse is so bad, why aren't they talking to them?

If they are married, then it's just that and they should be the ones ironing out their problems. If he doesn't want to be there, he should leave. And if he leaves without God's permission, he is still operating against God's will, and there are consequences when you step out of the will of God. Right there is where God has him and it is for a reason. I know this oh so well because in my first marriage, it was our thing, but God made it His thing. I know that it was the very best thing that could have ever happened to me. Without that marriage, I wouldn't be half the woman I am today. I wouldn't be half the wife to my now husband without that marriage. Without my ex, I wouldn't have the relationship with God that I have now. I mean that in a good way. There were things about myself that he taught me that no one else could. That's why our separating had nothing to do with no one else except us.

Women, if you simply stay in the will of God, he will allow you to be found. It breaks my heart when I hear a woman say, "I don't want to be married." Satan has caused today's woman to run from the commitment of marriage but operate in the operations of marriage.

Sinful Relationships

What am I saying? I've seen the same woman who claims she doesn't want to be married commit her body to someone else's husband or daughter (yes I said it), and live like they're married and do the things that married people do. The world and the devil that runs it, have produced an epidemic of harmful and sinful relationships. The church has closed its eyes, accepted it, and has often been the breeding ground for it. What does this have to do with His Mistress? EVERYTHING!!!

If you were living right or in a church that was preaching against some of these things, maybe, just maybe, you wouldn't be where you are right now. No one in the church, when I was young ever talked about fornication, cause everybody was fornicating. It was just as common for Pastors to have a mistress as anyone else. The church has been so committed to Kingdom Facility Building, until we have not only accepted members from Satan's kingdom that are still operating as such, but pastors as well. We must be concerned that people are truly getting saved!

Much Too Bold

I'll never forget a story my grandmother told me about when she joined this new church, the pastor's mistress told her, "Just don't mess with the pastor, because he's my man." I think I would have just turned around and walked out. How can a woman who is not even married to a man have the nerve to be protective of him? You see, sin will cause you to do some stupid stuff. Sin will also cause you to walk in a harmful boldness that could very well cost you your life.

I know because I rode in his cars, went to dinner with him, used his credit cards, and even sat up in his church. See what I'm talking about. You get bold. I'll never forget the time I was in the car with a married man, and we had a wreck. A car hit us and ran. The police officer spelled my name wrong, and that probably was the only thing that kept his wife from knowing that he had a woman in the car. This is the kind of action that could have cost me my life. You never know the mind set of another person.

Always know that one sin can cause you harmful reaction. You never know how the next person will act when they get angry. There is no covering for sin. I repeat, there is no covering for sin. When you are practicing sin, it is just like riding in a convertible with the top down. Your head and nothing else is covered. You walk completely out of God's safety zone when you decide to practice and live a life of sin.

This is exactly why sexual diseases are so rampant. Folks are sleeping with any and everybody! Even though you didn't get the enjoyment of sex with the previous persons they've slept with, you still end up sleeping with them when you sleep with the one who was there. We have neglected to keep ourselves under the safety zone of God's protection by deciding that it's about what we want. Don't you know that you really don't need everything you want? How is it that we believe that God will protect us in all of our mess? How much longer will grace abound?

In all of God's splendor and grace, through all of His love and provisions, there is still no justification for sin. *"The soul that sinneth shall and shall surely die"* (Ezekiel 18:4).

I am the first person to say, "Thank you Jesus for protecting me in my mess. Thank you Jesus for allowing me to see the light and change from my wicked ways." Sisters, it is not always on you. Men too need to take responsibility of their actions. You as a woman, have the authority to just say, "NO!"

LUKE 10:19

"Behold. I give unto you power to tread on serpents and scorpions, and over all the power of the enemy; and nothing shall by any means hurt you."

You have the power over the enemy right now, this day.

Please don't justify it by saying, "Well, I am not the one who went after him." Or the one I use to use, "I am not the one who's married. I'm not the one who made the vow and it's not my fault."

PROVERBS 30:19-20

19"The way of an eagle in the air; the way of a serpent upon a rock; the way of a ship in the midst of the sea; and the way of a man with a maid. 20. Such is the way of an adulterous women; she eats and wipes her mouth, and saith, I have done no wickedness."

You cannot continue in sin as if it is not your fault. You are just as at fault as the man you lay with. I know how you've invested your time, heart, and soul into this man. I know how he helps you financially. I know how you'd feel lost without him. I also know that there is one, Jesus, who if you invested the same time in Him, He could reestablish you and change your life. Being his mistress will not ever compare to the completeness you'll have from being God's daughter.

For those of you who feel that you can be anything you want to be, or do whatever you want to do, because you are truly covered under the blood of Jesus because you truly believe look at this...

1 CORINTHIANS 6:12 KJV

"All things are lawful unto me, but all things are not expedient: all things are lawful for me, but I will not be brought under the power of any."

So, I ask you the question…why would you want to be a slave to adultery and fornication? When you decide to live in sin, you decide to be a slave. Slavery is not just the bondage of African Americans in past history; it's exactly what you accept when you decide to allow your fleshly sins to control you. Don't let the mess in your life make you a slave.

Chapter Six

The Fate of His Mistress

From a biblical prospective let's review the story of Abram, Sarai, and Hagar in Genesis 16.

IN SUMMARY

"Now Sarai, Abram's wife, had borne him no children. But she had an Egyptian maidservant named Hagar; so she said to Abram.

"The Lord has kept me from having children. Go, sleep with my maidservant; perhaps I can build a family through her." Abram agreed to what Sarai said. So after Abram had been living in Canaan ten years, Sarai his wife took her Egyptian maidservant Hagar and gave her to her husband to be his wife. He slept with Hagar and she conceived. When she knew she was pregnant, she began to despise her mistress. Then Sarai said to Abram, "You are responsible for the wrong I am suffering. I put my servant in your arms, and now she knows she is pregnant, she despises me. May the Lord judge between you and me."

"Your servant is in your hands," Abram said. *"Do with her whatever you think best."*

Then Sarai mistreated Hagar; so she fled from her. The angel of the Lord found Hagar near a spring in the desert; it was the spring that is beside the road to Shur. And he said, "Hagar, servant of Sarai, where have you come from, and where are you going?"

"I'm running away from my mistress (the wife) Sarai," she answered. *Then the angel of the Lord told her, "Go back to your mistress (the wife) and submit to her."*

The angel added, "I will so increase your descendants that they will be too numerous to count."

The angel of the Lord also said to her: "You are now with child and you shall name hi Ishmael, for the Lord has heard of your misery. He will be a wild donkey of a man; his hand will be against everyone and everyone's hand against him, and he will live in hostility toward all his brothers."

It's My Right Too

As you read this story, doesn't it seem strange that Hagar would have to go through this even though Sarai offered her husband to her? To me, you would think that Sarai would be the one wrong, but it was Hagar. She allowed Sarai, in her unbelief, to get her caught up in her mess.

How many wives get other women caught up in their mess because they don't believe God?

I could go into the deepness of the Middle East confliction between those brothers, but its right here in the United States. Brothers are against brothers because he's the son of the other woman. Siblings fighting against one another for the sake of saying, they have their fathers name; thus accusing the illegitimate children as not belonging.

They're fighting for their birth-rights and the children are suffering due to the sins of their parents. So this is something else that you as a woman should think about when you decide to sleep with someone else's husband. If not for yourself, think about your children. Think about the young child that has to watch his or her daddy interact with their legitimate children while he or she is on the sideline watching. Think of the emotional turmoil that your child would go through. It's not easy for a child, wondering why their daddy doesn't love them. Think about it!

Chapter Seven

The Sin of Sex

I decided to take a walk through this subject, because I am finding more and more that there is a need for education in the church concerning sex. The church for so many years has failed to teach on the spirit and sin of fornication. Because of this, society has failed. There is such an epidemic of diseases surrounding and resting upon this world, because no one is strongly urging people against sex. Instead, commercials are telling folks what to use to make having sex easier.

Even when I chose to be his mistress, I was over twenty three years old and had yet to hear my first message about fornication or adultery. The only subject I'd ever heard was about David and Bathsheba, and they still didn't go deep enough for me to know that David slept with another man's wife. It was always about if David would have been at war where he was supposed to be, he would have never seen her. Sex is still such a forbidden topic in spite of the fact that everybody is doing it or thinking about doing it.

I use to think that it was such a cliché, because pastors were caught up in fornication and adultery just like the parishioners. In some cases you still see this in the church, and every day you see another pastor exposed for sexual sins in the church. But just like with anything else, you hear of those cases where it was swept under the rug and kept secret by the congregation in order not to destroy the church.

---

1 CORINTHIANS 6:13-18

13"*Meats for the belly, and the belly for meats: but God shall destroy both it and them. Now the body is not for fornication, but for the Lord; and the Lord for the body. 14And God hath both raised up the Lord, and will also raise up us by his own power. 15Know ye not that your bodies are the members of Christ? Shall I then take the members of Christ, and make them members of an harlot? God forbid. 16What? Know ye not that he which is joined to an harlot is one body? For two, saith he, shall be one flesh. 17But he that is joined unto the Lord is one spirit. 18Flee fornication. Every sin that man doeth is without the body; but he that committeth fornication sinneth against his own body."*

A Lesson On Love

I found this to be a question, is there a woman out there who truly loves herself? At a young age, girls are taught to love but whoever teaches her to love herself. I believe that their first lesson in love should be to love God and then their second lesson should be to love themselves. It's her love for God that will cause her to avoid sex, and her love for herself will cause her to understand why. She'll be totally aware that men use the word "love" to get sex, and won't feel the need to use "sex" to get love. This is totally against God's plan for relationships. It is not God's plan that you take your body, which belongs to Him, and have sex with a harlot, and it is not God's plan for you to be a harlot.

93

Don't think that women are the only harlots. The word harlot means prostitute, and these days you have men prostituting just as hard as women. It's not always a street thing either. You can easily become a prostitute by sleeping with everyone you date while expecting something in return. And yes you can prostitute for love instead of money.

---

1 CORINTHIANS 7:2

"Nevertheless, to avoid fornication, let every man have his own wife, and let every woman have her own husband."

This to me is the proof that you have a husband out there. If a husband is what you desire, just wait on God. Marriage is the institution that God designed. Not just for procreation, but to help you to avoid fornication.

I got to tell the truth, God dropped this into my spirit at five in the morning... "I don't always allow you to be found to satisfy your flesh, but to perfect and satisfy your spiritual man." God was telling me that my mate would be more help to me spiritually than he would be physically. Too many folks are marrying to satisfy their flesh, and when flesh satisfaction isn't enough in the marriage, then they venture own to the next person.

When our spiritual man is satisfied in marriage, *what do you mean?*

When we as women are found by a man that helps us connect to God through togetherness in the Word and he becomes a man (he loves his wife as Christ loves the church) by example of the Word, then this satisfies our spiritual man in the fact that we are now a threefold card—my husband, myself, and the Holy Spirit. Then, and only then, is when you'll have a real marriage.

---

1 CORINTHIANS 10:5-8

5"But with many of them God was not pleased: for they were overthrown in the wilderness. 6Now these things were our examples, to the intent we should not lust after evil things, as they also lusted. 7Neither be ye idolaters, as were some of them; as it is written, The people sat down to eat and drink, and rose up to play. 8Neither let us commit fornication, as some of them committed, and fell in one day three and twenty thousand."

This is a fair warning of the effects of sinning against our bodies. Just as in the days of Moses when these that fell (dead) because of fornication, people are falling dead by the thousands now because of fornication. So, think it not strange or something new; the fact that people are now dying from a disease contacted by fornication.

The Bible clearly states that the soul that sinneth shall surely die. God's word will not return unto Him void. He will not allow us to make Him out of a liar. There are deadly complications for disobedience. Your flesh and the lust of the flesh will cost you a life of damnation.

The church is so busy teaching you about prosperity, but someone needs to be teaching people how to live holy. If you live holy, you can withstand in evil days which we are living in. Dead folks don't need money, cars, or houses. The church needs to know about prosperity but more than that, the church needs to know how to accomplish soul prosperity. You'll never know real prosperity until you are living life according to the Word of God.

GALATIANS 5:19-21

19"Now that works of the flesh are manifest, which are these; Adultery, fornication, uncleanness, lasciviousness, 20Idolatry, witchcraft, hatred, variance, emulations, wrath, strife, seditions, heresies, 21Envyings, murders, drunkenness, revellings, and such like: of the which I tell you before, as I have also told you in time past, that they which do such things shall not inherit the kingdom of God."

Be Free

Some folks truly believe that all they have to do is believe in Jesus Christ, and they will inherit the kingdom of God. Is there anybody out there who's going to teach folks how to live holy? Is there anyone going to tell folks that you will not live any kind of way and make it to heaven?

There is a spiritual transference through sex. Diseases are spirits!!! They connect and breed through sex. That's why if you sleep with someone who is infected; the disease they carry is transferred to you. The sooner we understand this, the better off we will be.

Sickness is a spirit. Homosexuality and lesbianism is a spirit, and a choice to allow it to live through you. Yeah, I'm going here, because far too many folks have decided to blame God for their imperfections of the flesh. If you are right in what you are doing and how you are living, stop trying to justify it. Right folks don't need justification, but sin always tries to find a way to justify itself.

I have to be real with you because God has been real with me. He warned me that if I didn't turn from my wickedness, I would live life as a stray dog. Stray dogs don't get food unless it's from a dumpster. Can you imagine living like this? There are people in this world who are living all alone because of their choices. Our choices to sin can cause us a life of loneliness. Sin separates us from God, and without God, there is no cure from loneliness. What do I mean by separates us from God?

Sin Causes Separation

When I was fornicating at first I would repent after every act and try to shower to scrub myself clean to rid myself from the guilt of the sin. After so long, I started saying, "If God didn't want me to have sex, He wouldn't have made my body crave sex." And this is how the separation begins. We begin to take what God has created in purpose and make it justify our lustful acts. Then the more I spoke this, the more I believed it and repentance was no longer needed. See the separation. Words are powerful and when we speak them over ourselves...I was made this way....This is the way I am....I need it to thrive....our hearts begin to believe it and the more we believe our words, the more our hearts began to reject God's Word.

"Out of the abundance of the heart our mouths speaks" (refer to Matthew 12:34), and that's why we see folks on television talking about God made me this way. See, their separation from God has given them the authority to do them. Whatever is in your heart, your mouth will begin to speak. If you speak more of your words, that's what surrounds your heart, if you speak more of God's Word, then that's what surrounds your heart.

Not Just A Dream

In a dream a Prophetess came to my house to speak with some daughters of God, and as she began to justify homosexuality, I jumped in. I told her that this is a spirit that is trying to consume our flesh. Then I took her to Sodom and

Gomorrah when the angels came to Lots house and the men of the city both old and young tried to force Lot to turn the men over to them.

In the dream, the Lord had me to remind her that this spirit is not only forceful, it's demanding. They were demanding Lot to turn the men over so they could use them carnally. And as I began to explain this in the dream, she at first didn't believe me. I told her that I was molested by a woman. Instead of me giving in to the spirit that tried to force itself upon me, I started sleeping with every guy I came in contact with to prove to myself that I wasn't a lesbian or living with the spirit of homosexuality.

Do you know how many people are lesbians or homosexuals because someone forced themselves on them? The prophetess started to listen to me. Immediately, I got out of the bed and said, "Lord is this where I should go?"

Yes, I was molested at fourteen, and by a woman. My mother would let me go just about anywhere to keep peace in her home, and I ended up in the house of some folks where sexual sin was off the chain. One of the women that frequented there, woke me up on the sofa, and started doing things to my body and dared me to stop her. I can remember being so scared, and then she made me feel like it was my fault and if I told anyone she would tell on me.

As a result, of this, I couldn't even stand the smell of my own body. It drove me into a clean disorder to insure that I will never smell this smell again and infringed upon me a fornicating spirit that I accepted in order to prove to myself that I wasn't a lesbian.

Can you imagine carrying this weight at fourteen? I wouldn't have shared my experience of molestation even now if God hadn't awakened me in that dream.

So, when I got older and accepted my calling, I found that I was most interested in spiritual matters concerning demons and spirits and how they operate. And of course the first spirit that I needed to truly know and understand was the spirit of homosexuality.

Know What You Are Fighting

I began an in-depth study on Genesis 18-19. I had to know the spirit that I vigorously fought and why it had so much power over man. And enough power to make me come out fighting the only way I knew how, by having sex with men. God gave me first the characteristics of this city…enticing, perverted, carnal, mean, arrogant, forceful, intrusive, trickery, and wicked. In this, I could see the spirit that I began to fight at a young age. Go to Genesis and read now. See, these men both old and young were so perverse that as soon as these men came to Lot, they were determined to get them literally.

That's why this spirit of homosexuality and lesbianism rarely stops until it gets who it wants and it makes the ones who want to be free from it fight with all their might. The tenacity of this spirit causes one to either fight harder or simply gives in. It also causes a luring source that acts as a roper; once your weakness is displayed, it slowly pulls you in.

Lot offered his daughters, but they wanted no part of them. Of course, you see in the Word that the city was destroyed but not without Lot's future son-in-laws and his wife who looked back and turned into a pillar of salt. Now Lots' daughters who were the only ones to survive, put their own dad in a drug induced state and enticed him. Not just on one occasion but on two separate nights, to sleep with them both and they conceived sons born out of incest. So from one level to the next, these girls' sons were the byproducts of a spirit that lingered in one way or another. And get this, spirits are transferrable and just because the people of Sodom and Gomorrah were killed, doesn't mean that this spirit didn't lay doormat in one of the survivors.

We Wrestle Not Against Flesh And Blood

People of God, we have got to be more aware of the spiritual world. I asked why I was a target for this spirit. Then I remembered when my mother opened her doors to two girls who had no place to stay. After a while it was apparent that they were lesbians, and I hated them. As a child I couldn't understand why they would lie on God and say, "He made them this way." This angered me to the point of hatred, and it showed in my lack of reaction towards them. I didn't understand that sin was our nature and that God was a forgiving God who would forgive anything, but unbelief.

Children take what they hear to heart, and I'd taken to heart that this is not how women were supposed to be. So just as I detested this spirit, it detested me. The working of the enemy hasn't changed. He knows just who will destroy or speak against his plan, and so his objection is to destroy them.

I know this is deep for some, but people need an awakening to what is going on in the atmosphere.

EPHESIANS 6:12

For we wrestle not against flesh and blood, but against principalities, against powers, against the rulers of the darkness of this world, against spiritual wickedness in high places.

When the enemy can plant a spirit within us to harbor, it's specifically to destroy your witness. Above all, we were made to bring glory to God through our lives, actions, and understanding of His Word. If my lifestyle contradicts His Word, then I won't speak His Word so boldly or try to compel others by His Word.

So just as the enemy set out to destroy Christ from birth, his objective is to destroy the witness of the witness. That's why preachers and so many of those who are associated with the Word and the church fall prey to sexual sins. When we have sinned against our own bodies, it taints the heart of our minds (our soul) concerning our ability to bring forth a valid and strong witness. That's why David was so remorseful because of his actions towards Bathsheba and her husband (refer to 2 Samuel 12) and you hear this remorse in some of the Psalms of David. Sexual sins both break a witness down to bare necessity and cause him to remorsefully repent, or it will separate him from God.

The latter is the objective of the enemy and whether you know it or believe it, you better understand that just like God knows who you are, so does the enemy. God has given us the power to prevail but when our own bodies are tainted, it slows the process. The enemy knows that you are going to be a powerful television personality that the world will one day know and see. So he fights hard to taint you by causing you to accept one of his very own as a part of you (the spirit of fornication, lesbianism, adultery, etc.). So when you make it, there's no doubt that you have a good heart (always had) and you help the people.

Then the people accepted you, faults and all, because you do so much good. Then your gestures of goodness outweigh the grace of God that has allowed you another opportunity to repent and turn from your wicked ways. (You believe that as long as you do well by others, then you are okay with God and can live life how you want to. Thus in reality saying you are here because you do good and not because you have been given the grace to stay around until you transform your mind.) And Satan is at peace, because no matter how much good you do, you still are a part of him. And you rarely run into life troubles because it's a known fact that those who are lovers of this world enjoy the fruits of this world.

Can you see the enemy? You have been blessed with a platform where you can say, "God will save you, God will clean you up" and it will reach millions, but because you're living in sin, you don't care to discuss salvation. And as always your excuse is that the networks won't let you discuss religion. See how spirits rob us from giving God our all and bringing others to Christ.

Sharing Is Not Always Easy

In my book *Not Until You're Ready*, I talked a lot about my sexual sins. It was hard for me to disclose my personal life but I knew some young woman out there needed that information and the same is true with this book. Although I'm now living a life free of sexual sins, it's still not easy sharing my business. Fortunately, I understand that this thing is bigger than little ole me. Someone needs to know that they can be set free. I wouldn't care if someone showed naked pictures of me, because I was out there. There's no telling what they have from my past, but my past no longer determines who I am or my future.

My life is exposed and the spirits that otherwise would have chewed me for lunch are under the subjection of the prayers of the saints. Saints are praying that I don't fall, because my message wouldn't be as effective if you saw me in a gay relationship or heard of me sleeping with another man besides my husband. And because I know you are watching me because of what I write, it makes me accountable for my own actions.

I'll never forget when I came home and asked a teenage friend who has decided on a life of lesbianism…How do you get these girls? She said, "I wait for some guy who they depended on to break their hearts, then I start by buying their children some shoes. And the next thing you know she's telling me her problems, then I console her with a kiss."

I just thought that the females she entertained were just too girly for this type of relationship. And in her answer, I found the breakdown. The same spirit of trickery she used on them was the same spirit of trickery that this woman used on me. It's a play on emotions and if you admit it, our emotions can cause us to be caught up in sin so deep. If this happens, then I'll do this- it is trickery. Can't no one treat you like I can- it is trickery. Let me erase all of your pain- it is trickery. Now, don't get me wrong, not all lesbians or homosexuals were tricked into their lifestyles. Some willingly gave themselves over to that spirit.

A Free Moral Agent

That's why I'm on a mission to tell folks that there is more to life than sex! I would say to someone who is secretly dealing with sexual emotions that they feel are immoral to pray and find someone with whom you can talk too. Don't allow the enemy to define who you are, you are more than a conqueror through Christ Jesus. You can't live an abundant life in sin and with any other spirit other than the Spirit of the True and Living God. Spirits not only block you from becoming all you can be, they block happiness, joy, and completeness. We have the power to rebuke spirits that try to invade our lives. We must take authority first over our flesh.

I made the choice not to accept a spirit that was trying to invade my life and the choice to rebuke a spirit that took over my life, but not by myself. I had to asked the Holy Spirit to please come into my life and help me to live holy. No, I'm not perfect but I thank God that my sins aren't against my own body (sexual sins) anymore. And you better know that just because it didn't capture me, it vowed to linger in my lifeline, but I'm yet rebuking it in the name of Jesus and standing on the Word of God concerning my children, my grandchildren, my family, and my entire generation. We will be holy in both body and soul!

Now to those of you who are offended in one way or another by this chapter…get over it! I went through so that I can be a blessing to someone else and to tell you that you have a choice. You are a free moral agent who has the right to choose what is morally right for you. Whether your choice is a good choice or a bad choice, it's your choice and you have to stand before God in judgment for your own choices.

As for me and my house, we will serve the Lord, and our choices have been decreed over to be the choices that God has in place for our lives. Friend, the enemy has tried to get you and has now taken the distinct measures of attacking you through your flesh. Don't allow him to have authority over your flesh. Though you deal with this in secret, God has opened your heart to me, therefore I know the pain and torment that you are going through.

EPHESIANS 6:10-13 NIV

10"Finally, my brethren, be strong in the Lord and in the power of His might. 11Put on the whole armor of

God, that you may be able to stand against the wiles of the devil. 12For we do not wrestle against flesh and blood, but against principalities, against powers, against the rulers of darkness of this age, against spiritual hosts of wickedness in the heavenly places. 13Therefore take up the whole armor of God, that you may be able to withstand in the evil day, and having done all, to stand."

Deny your flesh and trust me, it is not hard to do. When you truly accept Christ in your life, things that once were hard become easy. I use to think I couldn't live without sex. I later found out that I could. The new man in you doesn't want any parts of sin. Untie yourself from the bondage of your flesh! YOU ARE FREE! And know that although the world is saying, "It's okay," God is saying, "It isn't."

A Prayer Against Sexual Sin

Father in the name of Jesus, I come to you now on the behalf of my sisters and brothers who are entangled in all kinds of sexual immortality. I pray now by the blood of Jesus that you will wash them and renew their minds and spirits, in the name of Jesus.

You died Lord for our iniquities, infirmities, sins, and diseases and because of this I believe we are able to withstand and conquer. You became a curse in order for us to be redeemed from the curse so now Lord I ask you to help us to walk in freedom from sin. Teach us how to claim the victory over our flesh. Heal us from all manner of sexual sins. We believe that we are free and that this prayer has been answered.

In Jesus Name, Amen.

Chapter Eight

Is the Spirit of Jezebel On The Loose?

Sharmen

Sharmen was sure that when she went into the job on the day after the kiss that she was dressed sexy enough to blow Mandery away. She'd chosen a sky blue pant suit that made her look like she was thicker on the rear end. She was going to make him regret the day he'd ever allowed her to taste those luscious lips of his. Sharmen kept replaying the kiss over and over in her mind. She still couldn't believe that it had happened and she was convinced that it would happen again and again.

One part of her was saying, "Don't take your heart through this pain anymore." Then again, there was a part of her desiring him like she'd desired no other. There was a void in his life and he'd made the mistake in letting her know it. She unlike some other woman was a willing and eager participant. In her mind, all she had to do was help him to see that whatever Christine was or wasn't doing, she wouldn't do or would do better.

REVELATION 2:20-23

20"*Notwithstanding I have a few things against thee, because thou sufferest that woman Jezebel, which calleth herself a prophetess, to teach and seduce my servants to commit fornication, and to eat things sacrificed unto idols. 21And I gave her time to repent of her sexual immorality, and she did not repent. 22Behold, I will cast her into a sickbed, and those who commit adultery with her into great tribulation, unless they repent of their deeds. 23I will kill her children with death, and all the churches shall know that I am He who searches the minds and hearts. And I will give to each one of you according to your works.*"

If you think what you are doing is something fun and just for play, you better take a deep look at the above passages. Right now at this very moment, God is giving some of you the grand opportunity to repent. Because you are so wrapped up in thinking you have so many more days to get it together, some of you will refuse to repent and miss the mark.

This Jezebel spirit is a trifling spirit that encourages the children of God to do wrong. This is an enticing seducing spirit that targets God's people. This spirit is not against the person whom it attacks, it's against God, and its major goal is to tear down your relationship with God. It is a spirit that will try to take you out.

This spirit says to the fornicator, it's alright to fornicate as long as you use protection. It says to the homosexual and lesbian, it's okay to sleep with another woman or man (of the same sex) because God made you this way. It says to the adulterer, it's okay to commit adultery as long as you don't get caught. Or even, you aren't the one who made a vow so in reality you aren't committing adultery. This might not always be what is said but know that if you are not disagreeing with the practices of either sin, then you are in agreement. And if you see me doing either of the things above, then I become a teacher of such practices.

You better recognize when this spirit is seducing you, or someone is teaching you to go against the infallible Word of God. I must say to you, our sin has nothing to do with God's love for us, because He still loves us. Nevertheless, our fight to remain from practiced sin is a true outward display of our love for God. And get this...He loves us so much that even in our mess, He'll still give us time to repent.

I'm not one hundred percent sure as to what goes on at the end of one's life, but in my time, I have seen evidence that the Word of God is true. I have seen a mistress cast into a sickbed and experience great tribulation. I am not sure as to whether or not she repented while on that bed of affliction, because only God knows. It is my prayer that she repented, but I see in this the grace of God. How can you see His grace in her suffering? No, I believe that God was just as hurt to see His child suffer through what she went through. However, He didn't allow the sickness to take her quickly. He kept death at a distant, and all I see in that is another opportunity for her to repent. We need to recognize when God's sufficient grace is giving us covering to come from under-cover operations.

I had a spirit of seduction so strong on my life until it was frightening for even me. You have to recognize this spirit and its length. A seductive woman can make the strongest man fall. I know because it seemed that the oar of seduction that fell on me is one that called out to influential men…God's personal servants. Now, I refuse to let them off the hook, because the whoremongering spirit that rested on them gave me an open invitation. When I went through my purification time, God allowed me to really study Jezebel. She was indeed an evil woman who wanted what she wanted, and did whatever she wanted to in order to get it. I began to repent and I begged God to take this spirit off me. It didn't vanish overnight but as time went on and I kept fighting for my soul to be free, I knew exactly when it had fallen completely off.

One night, one of the types of pastors whom I'd grown accustomed to, touched my head. My head began to hurt so badly. When I saw that spirit resting on him, I began to rebuke it in my mind. He quickly dropped his head, and hurried to the other side of the room. I knew then, at that moment that I was delivered. I also knew that the same authority that rested on me as a seductress was nothing compared to the authority that would rest on me as a Daughter of God. God cleaned me up so that I could take my rightful place as His Daughter, and then as the wife of His servant.

Now get this, I then had to make extra sure that this spirit was nowhere in my life. Why? Because this spirit is not only a seductive spirit, it is a manipulative, evil, persuasive, and controlling spirit. Whether you know it or not, this spirit is so prevalent amongst pastors' wives. I'm so glad that you are wondering how.

Example: Ms. Thang is a member of your church, and she speaks, and hugs pastor (your husband) just like everybody else. As a wife, you stop looking at the fact that she's Gods' child (flaws and all) and you start focusing on what she has on, and allow the spirit of jealousy and judgment and creep in. Then you tell him, "You better tell her to stop hugging you or I'm going to tell her myself. It'll be better if you did it instead of me!" However, this leads to the pastor avoiding his member in order to satisfy the spirit jealousy in you, because of the lack of trust in him.

Here's another example: "Baby, those deacons, and people are really messing with you at that church. I'm going to get a group of people to band against them because they don't know who they messing with." And now your husband is caught in the middle of a church feud with you directing, and planting seeds of discord.

Here's one for a wife who's not a first lady: "You better get your trifling, no good family members. They don't like me, and I don't like them. You better talk to your folks before I blow up on all of yall."

Or even this: You better get a backbone and go over there and tell those folks off.

Please don't forget this one: "You need to stop giving that church all of our money. It doesn't take all that to praise the Lord. You don't have to give that church nothing. Better yet you need to go see how Pastor bought that new car."

For the ghetto girls with the hard guy: "You don't need to be hanging with your friends all the time. Anyway, one of them tried to holler at me. They come right back, and tell me all of your dirt because they want me."

In each example, you see a wife stirring her husband to cause him to lash out in actions or in words. As a wife, you should never try to get a reaction from your husband by stirring his emotions. Get this; if the woman is in the church, and she's looking like a tramp, chances are she might still have some problems going on in her life. She needs the pastor, more than anyone, in order to help her to come to a point of change. A true man of God is mindful of the way the spirit of seduction operates, and he'll be the first to call the spirit out and rebuke the carrier of the spirit at the same time.

---

1 KINGS 21:23-25

23"*And concerning Jezebel the Lord spoke saying the dogs shall eat Jezebel by the wall of Jezreel. 24The dogs shall eat whoever belongs to Ahab and dies in the city and the birds of the air shall eat whoever dies in the field. 25But there was no one like Ahab who sold himself to do wickedness in the sight of the Lord, because Jezebel his wife stirred him up.*

You better make sure that as a wife you are not stirring your husband up to do something wicked, especially against God's people. I know oh too well how you feel concerning this too. It is almost like a wife's instinct to protect her husband and their relationship. I use to have it bad telling my husband, "Just because you let them make a fool out of you, don't mean I'm gonna let them make a fool out of me. So you better take care of the situation or I will. This is what I should have said, "Baby let me touch and agree with you concerning this matter, and believe God to make it better."

It is just not good to use manipulation; whether to get a man or to force your husband into doing what you want him to do. This is some serious stuff and Jezebel's tactics got her tossed out of a window and ate by dogs. This story is a must read for women, so that we will understand that our husbands authority is not ours. We also need to realize that God is watching us. It is an awesome thing being a woman, but it's even more of a blessing being a woman who strives in having a pure heart.

OTHER VERSES TO READ

1 KINGS 16:31, 18:4, 18:13, 18:19, 19:1-2, 21:5, 21:11, 14, 15, 23, 25

2 KINGS 9:7, 10, 22, 30, 36-37

REVELATION 2:20

Chapter Nine

Stop the Jezebel in Her Tracks

Christine

Christine could feel that the enemy was aggressively trying to bring separation into her home. She called Mandery and left a message on his phone, but he still hadn't returned her call yet. Christine believes in a God who could answer prayers so she did what she knew was the only thing to do; she prayed.

Father, I ask you now to forgive me for keeping secrets from my husband. Lord, you know my heart and know that I wasn't deliberately trying to disobey him. Please Lord, wherever he is, touch his heart. Satan, the Lord rebukes you now, in the name of Jesus. You have no place in my marriage, in my husband, or in our home. The blood of Jesus is against you concerning this marriage. Lord, I pray that you would bound the enemy as concerning this marriage that you put together and at the same time, I pray that you would renew the right spirit in the both of us. I love you Lord, and I stand on your word that says,

"Ask and it shall be given unto me." In Jesus name. Amen.

After she'd finished praying, she waited patiently for Mandery to come through the door. She believed by faith that the Lord would bring her husband back home where he belonged.

The way you stop the spirit of seduction from becoming a problem in your life, is by making sure everything around you is the way it should be. Sometimes our daily lives can become so filled with matters of life, until it becomes so easy to forget the things or people that matter the most. We are so overwhelmed with stuff, until we become burdened down and can't do the things we need to do.

Woman of God, just because God has delivered you doesn't mean that every female around you, or as a matter of fact, your very own husband, is delivered. I've found that the sure fire way to keep my husband from the clutches of this spirit is to keep him prayed up. I have an obligation to my spouse whether I want it or not. The largest task of me being a wife is making sure that he has everything he needs from every aspect. I must go here, because I see the spirit of seduction breaking into so many Christian families and tearing them apart. It is not just the fault of the husband, sometimes it's the wives fault as well. I've discovered in this walk, that all things must be done decent and in order and because of purpose.

Okay let's really talk now...

It amazes me how women pray for husbands and as soon as they get them, they don't want sex anymore. Before they became husband and wife, he could barely touch her, and she'd be ready for sex. Sex is so over-rated when you're committing fornication, but when you are married, it's under-rated. Can't you see the enemy? When sex is done right, (during marriage) it can be the most spiritual connection with a human (on earth) that you'll ever experience. Wives often loose the importance of this connection, and mostly they blame their loss of interest on their husband's greediness. Well ladies, I'd rather my husband be greedy with me than anyone else. And if I really get real with you,

I'd say, "He wasn't greedy when you were throwing it on him before you two got married." But yeah I know you only did that to get him.

If we really be real, there are a lot of things we do at the beginning of a relationship just to secure the connection. Nevertheless, it's these things that cause great affliction in our marriages. Don't do things before you get married that you aren't willing to do after you are married!!! I've seen so many marriages destroyed because of manipulation, deceit, and lies.

Not Obligated To, But I Desire To

I don't for the life of me, understand where wives get the notion that the only reason their husbands cheated with other women is because she was doing things the wife wouldn't. I guess this is said to make them feel better. You must understand that she could be doing the same thing as you, but instead of out of obligation, she's doing it out of desire. Obligated sex, and desired sex are two different levels. The number one excuse that I heard from the married man was in these words, "I have to beg her for sex, but she expects me to give her everything she wants freely." "She barely wants to have sex, and when we do she just lay there." Or, "She comes to bed like a missionary in those ugly gowns."

If you don't think this is important, ask your husband. Take off those flannel gowns, and wear the same gowns you wore when he was coming to your house before you got married. And to those of you who say, "I didn't wear any." Then I say, "Go back to that." I know this is too deep for some of you too holy women and that's why your husband is sleeping with the other women. Being holy is not just about being separated from the world, and set apart as for your belief. It's also about being set apart in your marriage, your parenting, and your everyday life. Your being set apart simply means your ability to do as the Word of God requires in spite of how the World teaches.

Marriage Takes Prayer

Now some of you married some men who aren't truly saved, and God's way doesn't seem to work. His greed is what causes him to require the affections of another woman. A glass half full always has room for more, and all I can say is sister hold on until God tells you to let go. Marriages take prayer to survive, and prayer changes things if you believe. So if you believe that God put your marriage together, it's time to fast and pray!! God has a way of bringing a whoremonger in, and sometimes they're not always going to be on their feet. You have to put that man in God's hands, and allow the one who created him to change him.

In the meantime, you be the wife that God has gifted you to be. Remember, there's nothing wrong with being submissive. It doesn't mean stupid, but it means allowing his authority to govern your home as he follows Christ. You would be surprised at how the seducer is able to seduce your husband because they come in the light of submission. They come willing to follow him as he leads. They ask his opinion before they decide to up and make changes. They are not concerned about losing him; their only concern is getting rid of you.

We derail the train of Jezebel when our husbands get the respect that is due to him, when we teach our children to honor the sanctity of marriage, when we teach our daughters to love God and themselves, and when we through fasting and prayer strengthen ourselves to stand against the enemy for our husbands.

Chapter Ten

What Women Need To Know

Mandery

Mandery drove slowly towards his house. All he could think about is what he'd just done. It had only taken one second for the enemy to make his thoughts overpower everything he knew was right. He'd known that he hadn't been in prayer like he should have been, but lately with work and Christine's spending, he was overwhelmed.

When he really thought about what he'd just done to Christine, a lonely tear strolled down his cheek. He'd never in a million years thought he'd see the day that he would allow himself to cheat on his wife. It was a kiss of passion and he shouldn't have ever felt this type of passion for any woman other than Christine. He no doubt created a mess and now he had to figure out how to solve his problems.

His father cheated on his mother constantly and he'd made a vow never to cheat on his wife after he saw his mother on the floor balled up in a knot crying her heart out. He wouldn't dare put the mother of his child through what his mom had gone through. Now he had to fix this mess and he knew he couldn't do it by himself. So he began to pray as he drove home.

Get Away From That Man

First although you think you are, you aren't even fascinated with him. If you really knew him, you probably wouldn't even like him. It so astonishes me how the enemy plays with our minds and emotions. We are so misinformed concerning the work in progress in our souls until we consent to our souls governing our affairs. And when we fall prey to forbidden relationships, our souls become the chief advisor. As a woman, I was so unaware of how I reacted by what I felt, quicker than I did by what was reality. If I thought I was lonely, I tried to find friendship. The reality was I was never alone at all; the Spirit of the Living God was always there. Stop allowing this spirit to usher you into painful, immoral, demonic relationships.

When we get involved with married men, it is not an attack on just us; it is an attack on him as well. For centuries the enemy has used women to kill the very essence of the male. You find a broke down brother and I can almost guarantee you that most of the time, at the root of his heartache is his wife, his mother, or his lover. Don't get me wrong, I need you to understand the power of persuasion and suggestion that a woman has over a man. Yes, they have their own minds, but our minds are far more advanced and skilled in deception than theirs. And we have the tool that the straight man loves to use.

Skilled In Deception

Our minds' advancement over theirs and our tool plays a huge part in man's fall. You take a married couple, for instance, who's cheating. The male usually gets caught, and the woman could have been the one who starting cheating in the beginning husband will never know. Some of you reading this book are the ones cheating and not your husbands and they don't have a clue. Why? Because just as the enemy beguiled Eve before Adam, the same is still in motion. The enemy has greatly impressed upon women the power of deception that will bring a brother to confession, and he doesn't even know he's confessing. You can make him tell all his business as you plot to destroy him instead of helping him.

My Brother's Keeper

Our men have since the Biblical days gotten caught in many situations trying to prove or impress us. Some of our brothers are locked up right now, trying to prove to some woman, that he wasn't weak. It's amazing how the jails and the graveyards are so heavily populated with men and the general population seems to have closed their eyes and minds to this. I write this to spark a reality check concerning Satan's fury against the male. Even throughout the Word of God, you'll find where men were the suggestive targets of the enemy. This has not changed. If Satan can destroy the male, his integrity, his life, his character, and his will power, then he's already destroyed you. We must keep in mind that we were created from man.

Women should know that whether directly or indirectly, if Satan bothers our brothers, we are affected too. Not only are we affected, but the church, our children, and our society is affected also. You wonder why there are more women in the church than men, you wonder why women are raising their children alone, go figure. Can you see the plot?

Satan's Device

Because of how the male is designed, Satan uses sex as one of his greatest devices towards men. It is no secret that the male sexual appetite is far greater than the female. I'll never forget when I first got married and I told my great-grandmother, Mrs. Odessa Murray, that I was so sick of my husband because all he wanted was sex, sex, and more sex. This is how she replied. "That's what's wrong with yall young folk's marriages now. You better understand quickly that he doesn't speak the same language as you. He solves his problems when he comes home and has sex with his wife. Gal, you better give that man some before somebody else gives it to him!"

My first response was to argue the point that he would be wrong if he did. I told her that just because I won't give him sex is not enough reason for him to run to another woman. I even argued that if he did go off with another woman, he wasn't meant to be my husband in the first place. She quickly pulled out her Bible and took me here…

---

1 CORINTHIANS 7:1-5 NIV

1"Now for the matters you wrote about: It is not good for a man not to marry. 2But since there is so much immorality, each man should have his own wife, and each woman her own husband. 3The husband should fulfill his marital duty to his wife, and likewise the wife to her husband. 4The wife's body does not belong to her alone but also to her husband. In the same ways, the husband's body does not belong to him alone but also to his wife. 5Do not deprive each other except by mutual consent and for a time, so that you may devote yourselves to prayer. Then come together again so that Satan will not tempt you because of your lack of self-control."

I wish that pastors would teach these scriptures in marriage counseling before they marry couples. Infidelity is one of the main causes of divorce. Although marriage means so much more than just having sex, I must tell you that sex is a vital part of marriage. And when you neglect this vital part, it causes problems. Remember that just because God has brought you under the power of self-control, doesn't mean that your husband is there. For some reason, we feel that people ought to be where we are in Christ. He has a season for each of His children and we are on God's timing. Some things that we walk into the grace of understanding concerning are made manifest, because we were ready to receive. Don't think he ought to know things or feel things, just because you know and feel them. One of my worst downfalls in marriage has been trying to read my husband according to what I thought. My thoughts aren't his thoughts, just like God's thoughts aren't our thoughts.

Two minds might come up with the same concept, but two minds just don't function alike. The connection that brings our minds together is pursuing a mind like Christ's. Women, we are not mind readers, so it is better to ask questions than to assume answers. My great grandmother had much more wisdom in her at seventy nine years of living than I, and I had no right to present a rebuttal. (In January 2010, Odessa Murray made 101! And she's still alive...Praise God for her wisdom!)

Self-Control, Do You Have It?

We must remember that it's our lack of self-control that causes us to fall into the trap of lust. For so many years, Satan has used the lack of self-control to destroy the witness of so many of God's men. So many affairs begin with people who don't have self-control and people who are not in the right position. It is important that you be in the right position in your life and in your marriage. Positioning starts with hearing and obedience. The ability to hear God, obey God, and then having enough self-control to stay on track. Women we must stay in God's way and in His will and He'll direct your paths. Our men need us to recognize the tricks of the enemy concerning them. We must take a moment to see how the enemy is operating against God's men.

The Enemy In Operation

It saddens me so when I hear of young men dying every day. I think about the wife who is left with no husband, the child with no father, and the mother without a son. The lack of male presence in our lives has caused a worldwide issue called single parenting. And for some children, divorce is so similar to death of a parent.

When marriages are broken, children are broken, and when children are broken, their futures are sometimes broken. When or if we are deliberately causing pain to someone's family, we don't think about what the children are feeling. I keep going back to the children, because working at a school has shown me how much family really matters. I see the happiness of children who have a two parent household verses the independency of children raised by a single parent. It is like the children in the one parent home grow up so much quicker. Not only that, it is hard for them to adjust to the authoritative voice of a male. I have seen when single parents get married, how the children rebel.

We as adult women need to stop thinking about ourselves, and begin or start thinking about our children. It is so crazy how we get married, start families, leave a husband, and then long to have a husband. We don't paint finished portraits, but instead we start and stop as we go. I can't say it enough how I thank God for the earthly father he blessed my children with. Their dad not only stayed around, but he had done just as much parenting as I have, if not more. When we got caught up in worldly things that led to divorce, we never forgot about our children. So for me, it wasn't hard for me to drop the child support case in support of him going through some rough times. I understood that his being there physically for our children was much more than finances any day. There are so many children apart from their fathers because of money and that's exactly how the enemy wants it. If he can bring animosity amongst the parents concerning money, then the children grow up feeling like they couldn't depend on their dads, and for boys this is horrible.

We all need to be in repair mode. Broken marriages or relationship, but we can be fixed by God. And when He fixes us, we must fight to stay mended so our children will believe in love and in marriage. It is so amazing how we fight so much harder to make our second marriage work.

Let me go back here because I want you to fully understand the fight for our men. I'll never forget when I was told that I was pregnant for the third time. Satan quickly reminded me that I already had two children and we were a young military couple having enough problems already. I came home from Japan to abort the baby. As I sat in the clinic, I looked around at all the young teenage girls. I couldn't help but feel like I was in the wrong place. This was Satan's first attempt to kill my son. After leaving the clinic and deciding there that I was going to keep my baby, two months into the pregnancy and I begin to threaten miscarriage. This was Satan's second attempt. Then when the baby was born a month early, and we later found out he had lung problems resulting in asthma. This was his third attempt to kill my son. Yes, the devil is a liar!

I know that my son was no different from the Egyptian baby put in a basket and in the pond for protection. I had to put him under the power of prayer and plead the blood of Jesus over him. I am teaching my son how important it is to be a man of integrity with his father, and step father, leading the way by example. I'm to my son, just like the mother in Proverbs teaching her son the true characteristics of a virtuous woman. Just like I'm teaching my son what to look for in a woman,

I'm teaching my daughters how to become women of standard and virtue.

I'll Teach My Own Children

Infidelity has become so rampant, until society teaches our daughters how to accept being the other woman. Secular music instructs them how to cheat with someone else's man, and it also teaches them how to accept a cheating mate. It teaches our sons that it's okay to have more than one woman and a night with him will make other's daughters think he invented sex. Listen to what your children are listening to. It is better to be informed so you can counter attack the tricks of the enemy. This world denotes that infidelity is a way of life, and that it's natural and okay. Not only is infidelity promoted, but adultery as well. We must combat what is learned in society by teaching our children what is right according to God's Word.

You don't know how hard I had to hide sin, to keep my children from seeing their mother in sin.

When my children read my books concerning

my sinful relationships, they were surprised. I thank God that He gave me enough sense not to bring any and everybody over my children. I didn't want my children calling everybody uncle, when in fact it was just my man. Protect your children from everything you possibly can!

Know Who You Are

Women you need to know that you are God's helper for man. Stop destroying men by allowing them to use you for the sole purpose of fornication. If women would just say, "No," a whole lot of things would change.

Don't compromise!

---

1 CORINTHIANS 7:1-5 NIV

9But you are a chosen people, a royal priesthood, a holy nation, a people belonging to God, that you may declare the praises of him who called you out of darkness into his wonderful light. 10Once you were not a people, but now you are the people of God; once you had not received mercy, but now you have received mercy.

Don't compromise what you know, and who you are in Christ Jesus. No matter what the enemy tries to break into your emotions with, don't compromise. Even if it seems to be the answer to an easier way, don't compromise. No matter how you've been praying for a mate, and it seems like he's not coming, don't compromise. God has a plan in store for you women of God, and He will take care of you and the circumstances of your life. It's going to be alright. Even to you, who might be in the very act of adultery, tell that brother that you won't compromise anymore. Cry and move on to see just what the Lord has in store for you.

In order to help our brothers, we have to learn to help ourselves. In order to fix our brothers, we have to be willing to fix ourselves. Not by ourselves but with the help of the one who can save and change anybody. Then as older women, we must live so that we can teach our younger sisters the way.

Chapter Eleven

What Young Women Need To Know

Mandery & Christine

Mandery dried his weeping eyes and went into the house. Christine greeted him with a hug and a kiss on his cheek. With unspoken words, she led her husband into their living room where she had pieces of paper strolled all over the sofa and coffee table. She had a yellow ledger lying on the table with numbers from top to bottom.

"Mandery, first of all, I owe you an apology." As Mandery got ready to interrupt her, she held one finger to his lips. "Here is an outline of all the money that I have spent this year. Mandery, as you see here, I've been buying those expensive purses and some other things for the women's shelter on Texas Avenue."

"You've been doing what?"

"My mother use to tell me that it wasn't good enough for me to walk around with designer bags like I was all that, and never give one to someone who would want it and can't afford to buy it. I never told you that I was giving those things away, because my mother also said you don't do something for someone and boast about it. I know I should have told you, but I just didn't think it would matter."

"You mean to tell me that you be giving those purses away. Is that why I only see them once?"

"Yes baby, because the very next day, I take them to the shelter. I also give them a wallet and put a little money in it. As you see here on our tax papers, I file all of our charitable deeds and as it turns out, our giving becomes a blessing for us."

"Baby, how could I have ever thought that you were being selfish? I know the kind of woman I married, but it just seemed like you were getting caught up in how much money the firm was making."

"Mandery, you ought to know me better than anyone. I'll never do anything to try to impress anyone except you. I've never been caught up in stuff but I believe stuff sometimes make people who can't ordinarily buy them, happy."

"Christine, I apologize for ever doubting you. There's something that I must tell you. I shared a kiss with Sharmen. I was so caught up in the fact that you defied me concerning the sofa that I allowed the enemy to entice me to do what I had an evil desire to do. Baby, I am so sorry for what I've done. I almost threw my marriage away, behind an assumption."

"The sofa came from Good Will and I cleaned it up so I could give ours to the shelter but now I don't know if any of this was the problem in the first place. Maybe, your desire to be with another woman was the root to you trying to find something on me."

"Christine, I promise it wasn't that. Baby, I could have hid the fact of what I've done, but I know that I was dead wrong. I will take care of the mess I've started, and I promise you that God has already dealt with me. His punishment is why I want to be truthful with you."

Don't Become a Duck

This chapter is for that young blood that's going around telling her home girls that she found herself a duck. Have you ever been to a duck pond? Those ducks will perform for you as long as you are giving them some bread. As soon as the last piece of bread is tossed out, they'll hang around for a little while longer to see if you'll throw out anymore. As soon as they get the notion that you won't be putting out anymore, they'll go back to doing exactly what they were doing before you came...huddling with their duck family.

So don't get it twisted lil' momma, in the end you'll be the one who have gotten used. A dollar a day might make you stay, but it surely won't keep the doctor a way. The same brother that paid your bills, and gave you a little change, who you thought was a duck- could very well turn out to be a duck trainer and you, will be the duck. Don't think that a man is going to leave his family, because you gave him some of your body. It takes more than sex to make a man leave his wife. You've probably had a friend or two that is now married to the married man they were cheating with, so let me drop this on you.

Most men hate to be alone. He didn't leave his wife for her. He was already making adjustments to leave his marriage. He simply secured a nest before he left, so he wouldn't have to build a new nest by himself. More than likely, his wife is the one who decided to leave him, and you just happen to be the one whom he knew would cushion the fall. I must serve notice that the same problems he had in his first marriage, will began to filter into his second marriage. Why? It's because he didn't have the opportunity to get his soul cleaned or free. Stop allowing old junk to fester in on you, and stop being the junk yard for men who haven't been fixed, healed, or changed.

Watch Out For the Trade-In

You know how folks start having problems with their car, they trade them in. You go out there looking for a cheap car, and you walk on the very lot and to the very car they just traded in. You pay your down payment, take the car home, brag about how pretty it is, and how dependable it will be. Well, it's a month later and that pretty, dependable car has already had to have tires changed, a new oil pan, and more fan belts. You try to deal with it, because it is yours and you're still paying for it.

You then notice a little pulling, but decided it just needed a tune up. You got the tune up and a few weeks later, when you put it in drive; you realize that the transmission has gone out. Not only will the car not move, it starts leaking transmission fluid like crazy. Now your driveway is stained with the fluids left from this not so pretty car that has proven to be not so dependable after all.

The moral of the story is...*Don't be so quick to pick up a man that another sister has just traded in.* And, don't let that brother run to you for a safe haven until he figures out it really wasn't you whom he was looking for. If you don't allow that brother time for God to fix, heal, and clean him up, you'll be inheriting the same problems that made the other sister trade him in. Give him an opportunity to see the era of his ways. If not, you'll be paying with your heart, to have the mess he leaves you to clean up, after he is long gone.

Help a Young Sister Out

Older folks this was a timely message for the young women, but you could use it as well. Some of you are still cleaning us messes you made when you were their age. Help these younger women to understand what state they are in. You can't keep hiding where you've been by keeping silent, open up and help them. Sometimes they need to know that you've been in the same place they are now in.

Young women, enjoy your life now. You have such an awesome opportunity to be found by a young man who is saved both body and soul. I'm watching a new thing in this new generation, and the young men are staying pure and are looking for wives who are pure. I need you to know now that being fine, having lots of money, and having a man won't make you happy. You won't find true happiness, until you understand that everything you need is waiting on you. As your soul prospers, you'll see prosperity in other areas of your life.

His Money Ain't Worth Your Time

I want young women to be aware of men who are infuriated with women being their equal, and result to ruining their lives because they haven't had the experience. They claim to want a younger woman for the things that she makes his body do. My thing is, sometimes your body doesn't need to do anything but rest. I think of all the older men I've seen wrapped up with a young woman. On television right now, there is a show of an old man with young women. I feel sorry for the young women who get caught up, and waste their lives hoping that this man will marry them. They could be somewhere living life to the fullest but instead, they're entertaining this old fart by doing things they probably wouldn't ordinarily do. Mothers, we must teach our daughters not to allow money, men, and manipulation through power to make them sell out.

She that hath an ear let her hear what the spirit says to the women!

Who Do You Believe You Are?

Often it is what a young lady thinks of herself that will cause her to run from the status of a mistress, or else run to it. When she has been taught that she is more than that, she won't accept that. If she thinks that she's fit to be the wife of one man, she won't accept anything less than that. If she believes that she is the royalty of God, she wants to be treated like royalty. If she believes that she is highly favored and blessed of God, she's going to operate like she is.

PROVERBS 23:7

"For as he thinks in his heart, so is he."

Chapter Twelve

What Wives Need To Know

Sharmen

Sharmen came in the office and the first thing she noticed was the note taped to her computer. It read....Ms. Sharmen please come directly to my office when you read this letter. Sharmen put her bag down and braced herself for another big kiss from Mandery. When she knocked on his office door, she heard a female voice say, "Come in."

Sharmen was shocked to see Christine sitting behind Mandery's desk. She could see that Christine was amused by her look of surprise. She had to regroup because she knew something was about to go down.

"Sharmen, I didn't mean to startle you. I see you were expecting Mandery."

"Yes, I was but it's nothing."

"You are exactly right, it is nothing. I understand that you and Mandery shared a kiss and it is my place to inform you that it will never happen again."

"Yes, but."

"There is no but. It was my first thought to fire you but I understand how any woman can be taken by Mandery. I also understand that Mandery was more at fault than you for allowing it to happen. So, I've decided to move you to the west end office to be Mrs. Johnson secretary, because I just don't think that your being here is what is good for you are Mandery."

"I can't afford to lose my job Christine. So, I don't have any other choice but to go."

"I appreciate your cooperation. I don't dislike you, but I understand the spirit that is trying to rest on you. I promise you Sharmen that being the mistress of a married man is not something you want to be. I don't care if you've seen it work with someone else, God is not pleased."

"How did you know? How did you know I've watched this kind of relationship all my life?"

"The spirit of God shared with me that this might be the case. It's because of God that I'm not hostile. I just

believe that I can help you Sharmen. I don't know what you've had to deal with or even what you are dealing with right now, but I do know that God is a forgiving God. In order for me to be forgiven, I have to forgive you. I would like you to attend women's prayer with me on Tuesday at noon. I've already made preparations for you to attend with me if you like."

"Christine, I would need to think about it. Thanks for not firing me." Sharmen said and quickly left the room.

Christine's ability to show her true forgiveness kept Sharmen from feeling so furious. She felt like Mandery could have warned her, but she understood that they were a family. She still couldn't help feeling shameful.

When I was the mistress, these were my special qualities:

- I listened more than I talked.

- I always wore something sexy that looked nice.

- I always cooked whatever he suggested.

- I was available for sex at his beck and call.

- I allowed him to give his money.

- I never criticized or raised my voice.

- I believed in his dreams and visions.

- I always greeted him at the door.

- I gave back rubs and bubble baths.

- I listened to him complain about all you didn't do.

It Takes All That

I don't know if you noticed or not, but some of these things you use to do, but stopped as soon as you got married. It's crazy how we are programmed to do all the good things to get the man, and as soon as we get him, we begin to treat him like old junk. And I believe that this happens because we go into relationships being fake. If you're not going to continue doing nice things, don't start doing them. It's better to never take upon yourself the responsibility of caring for a man, than to start them and later neglect them. I am not the only one who has neglected my responsibilities as a wife! If you were truthful with yourself, you could probably admit that you have too. It's like the uninformed Christians say, "It don't take all that to praise the Lord." And those of us who know what God have done- we say, "Baby, it takes all of that and more." I'm saying the same thing is required concerning taking care of your husband…it does take all this and more. If you find a couple that's been married for some years, notice how the wife makes sure that her husband is well cared for. She's more concerned about his needs than her own.

The Old Way That Still Works

I will never forget when I was in my first marriage, and we'd come home from Japan to visit our parents. My mother-in-law would be home cleaning, and as soon as her husband whom she affectionately called, Brother David, hit the door, she had his meal on the table before him. He'd greet his wife and the rest of us who were around, wash his hands, and sit down to a home cooked meal. Then, he'd take his bath and freely sit down for some evening time with the Lord. I noticed that no matter how her day went, if she hadn't told him everything during dinner time, she'd wait patiently until he'd spent time with the Lord. Normally, while he was enjoying his Bible, she would be in the back ironing his t-shirts and boxers that she'd washed earlier.

Her Way Wasn't the Crazy Way, but Mine Was

I can remember thinking this woman is nuts! Who in their right mind iron their husband's t-shirts and boxers? I thought she did all this because she was bored, and then I asked. She responded by telling me that because Brother David works so hard for his family and for the church folks (where he was the pastoral leader), the least she could do was make sure that he was taken good care of at home.

Now, in all the days I knew my father-in-law, I'd never once heard about him being with another woman. I'd never heard about him disrespecting his wife or neglecting her financial, emotional, or spiritual needs. I just wish that I would have seen back then, what I see now through spiritual eyes. I instead watched her through the eyes of a young selfish woman. If anybody was going to be ironing some boxers, it would be him and not me.

Things have changed for me now that I'm on my second marriage and I'll do whatever it takes to let my husband know that I love him. Most of all, I go an extra mile to show him that I appreciate him. That's all Mrs. Emma Gatlin was doing back then. She was showing her Brother David how much she appreciated all he'd done for her and their children. Every day was another opportunity for her to show her husband just how much she loved him. See, we must understand that love is an action word. It is not so much of what you say, more than what you do. Everything she did, though crazy to me, was remarkable for him. And I am more than sure that she was one of his greatest inspirations.

I'm not saying that if you don't do these things, he won't stay. What I am saying is that everything I stated above represented caring and catering to his desires and making sure that his cares and needs are your cares too. I've noticed in my second marriage that the reality of his provision or not being able to provide is sometimes over whelming to him. I have my mind on what I want, and he's got his on what we need. Most of his wants are never expressed and never purchased unless I purchase it. So sometimes could loving him symbolize to him that I appreciate him in good times and bad times; when we have plenty and when we have nothing? Could going the extra mile show him that he's totally appreciated? Could taking care of his clothes like Mrs. Gatlin show him that I'm even concerned about the smallest, most intimate details where it concerns him? Sure!

A Godly Man

Wives need to know that there is a blessing in having a good man, but there is a divinely extra special blessing in having a Godly man! A Godly man far outweighs a good man, because he does things the Godly way. He's concerned about you so much, until he'll risk everything to care for you.

He's not concerned about what folks say, or about whether his family likes you are not. He's concerned about his wife. He loves her as he does himself. He's even willing to do the dirty jobs that she needs him to do. If you ever get sick, women of God you better pray you have Godly men. He doesn't mind wiping your butt when you can't. He'll clean up the messiest mess and won't think twice. He'll do for you everything that you'll do for your child.

The Importance of Sex in Your Marriage

Check this divine revelation that God gave me concerning sex with my husband...

Notice how serious God is about the tithe. God blesses us to have jobs, He takes care of us, He loves us, and all He asks us to do is love Him enough to not touch what belongs to Him. However, when we do touch the tithe, we bring ourselves under the power of the curse. Not that God wants us cursed, but we ought to love God enough not to want to take what is His, and love ourselves enough not to be under a curse.

See, to your husband, your body is sacred and is his. It's like the tithe in your marital relationship. You can share everything else: your time, your talents, your love, etc. while in the marriage, but it is one part that is sacred only unto your spouse. It's the marital tithe. When you neglect to come together you place yourselves in the eye of the curse of failing self-control.

---

1 CORINTHIANS 7:3-5

"Let the husband render to his wife the affection due her, and likewise also the wife to her husband. The wife does not have authority over her own body, but the husband does. And likewise the husband does not have authority over his own body, but the wife does. Do not deprive one another except with consent for a time that you may give yourselves to fasting and prayer; and come together again so that Satan does not tempt you because of your lack of self-control."

Whether you realize it or not, sex matters. My aunt once said, "I wish I would have known to just give him some." She said that is all her husband wanted, and she was too ignorant to know it. No, sex won't solve problems, but lack of sex could very well create problems in your marriage.

Mandery

Mandery had heard of the confrontation between his wife and Sharmen. He didn't expect anything less from his wife. Christine had always been a God-fearing woman, and she was created with integrity and class. He'd known all too well that Christine would take this situation as an opportunity to help this young single woman find herself.

He had taken the liberty to buy his wife several dozen of roses, and made the house out of the romantic place she'd created it to be. He wanted nothing more than to just love the woman he'd almost destroyed with his selfish act. Nothing would stop his apology, and he refused to let his apology be in words only.

Danyelle Scroggins

It Pays To Be Nice

Think about most of the married couples that you know. If the husband is an exceptionally nice guy, the wife is sometimes the meanest person. Of course, this is sometimes vice versa. I ask this question often…who wants to live with someone who acts like they can't stand themselves. Mean people are the hardest people to start and maintain a productive family with. It might seem like it works, but I promise you that your spouse feels battered every day.

The worse person, I feel, on Earth to live with is a mean woman. She will cut you so bad with words, until you feel less than who you are. Mean people have put up a defense to keep themselves from getting hurt and it usually starts in their face. My pastor the late Pastor Arthur Washington use to say, "You look so mean like you have a jaw full of wasps." He was exactly right. Mean people can't help but look mean. Generally, what you feel inside is bound to show up on the outside.

Women, we need to learn that our attitudes can make or break our marriages. My grandmother use to tell me, "Girl it doesn't cost you nothing to be nice, but being mean can cost you everything you've got including your life." I thank God for the late Sister LB Ford and her words of guidance and instructions. She's gone home with the Lord, but her words are forever etched in my heart. So much so, that even if I get angry, God will allow someone to whisper to me, "Be nice."

There's a lot that I can't tell you concerning a man because I'm not a man, but as a woman, I can tell you that being nice will gain you much more from a man. A marriage is meant to be a fun and relaxing institution. Nevertheless, some men are experiencing this not in their own marriage, but instead with their mistresses. Why is this? Because at home the air is so thick with hatred, mean attitudes, and problems and his mistress always provides a problem free, stress free environment. I know that some women are saying, "Yeah, because they don't have to bother with these bills and these children."

Danyelle Scroggins

She Might Be Singing His Praise

I need to tell you wives, that most of the time, they have bills and their own children. He's just more apt to help them pay her bills and take care of their children, because taking care of their things gives them pleasure. How? She's never ashamed to thank him for being her KING. I need to let you know that some mistresses do get the man. Why? Because some of them are so happy about having someone in their lives until they perfect the ...I'll honor you, I'll do whatever you want, I'll take care of you.... and the brothers feel like they're in the place thy should be. So wives I urge you to, fix things in your marriages.

I have incorporated some of the traits that I enhanced while being a mistress, but nevertheless, I had to hit the storm before I did them. I was just like some of you, in a stale, same every day routine in my marriage. Wake up, freshen up, go to work, come home, cook a meal, watch a little television, and then go to bed. In between these actions, we might tell each other what needs to be done, paid, or what the children did or need. We neglected to say to one another, "Baby, I need you…" It was so bad until some days when he'd made it home, I'd already be asleep and wouldn't see him until the next day. Does this sound familiar? Are you like I use to be? Knows what he needs to be doing and thinks that if he does what he needs to do, then you'll do your part. Well sister, don't wait on him to do his part, do yours.

If you want romance in your marriage, initiate it! It is funny how Satan always put barriers in your mind to stop you from doing what you know is right to do. But don't be in sin!!!! When you're in sin, Satan is constantly giving you ways to make it better. "Secret Sex" is all Satan offers and this type of lustful sex will dig a ditch for you, and smother everything good. Don't be guided by that smut. Take authority over your marriage and take care of your man. Make your own bedroom that is already ordained by God, a romantic oasis. Take that television and those phones out of your bedroom. Your bedroom is a resting place for you and your man. Sometimes, we go to bed better with our friends (on the phone), than we do with our husbands. My husband use to have to listen to me blab all night on the phone until he fell asleep. If you allow everything to go on in your bedroom, you'll soon see that nothing is going on in your bedroom!!!

Love Is The Key

Before you can make any changes women of God, in your marriages, you must learn how to love. Love or lack of love is sometimes the reason why we suffer so much in marriage. I use to tell my husband, "I wish that you would care about me because if you ever stop loving me, if you care, you won't do me any ole kind of way." Well sisters, I don't say that anymore. I am singing a new song, "Lord, tell me how, and what I need to do to make him love me like you love the church." On the other hand, I need to embrace his love like the church has embraced Jesus love for it. Or has the church embraced it? I say that because, one of the hardest things for us to do is except that Jesus does loves us. Nevertheless, regardless to how hard it is for us to except, He has already proven His love because He died for us. Now, it's up to us to embrace this fact and then learn how to love as He loves.

Repetition Can Kill

Look at this... Have you ever been in a dead church? A church that seems like the presence of God is far from it. A place where everything has become ritual and traditions has taken over; this is a prime example of a church that doesn't understand the power of God's love. When you know the power of God's love for you, you will allow His spirit "Free Flow." Our marriages can be just like this...far from the presence of love and filled with rituals and repetitious events. I hate going to this type of church and so now you can see why your husband hates coming home to this type of marriage. Remember that your home is an extension of the church and your church has the essence of the home, because you my dear are the church. Love should be the most vital part of you...you the church, you the wife. Both parts of you were created in love and should be sustained by love. You are the Kool-Aid, he's the water, and love is the sugar that makes it taste so good.

Love (John 3:16) gave us a second chance at life and this same LOVE can teach you how to love and renew your marriage if you put HIM first (Matthew 6:33).

Christine & Mandery

Christine thanked the Lord all the way home from the office. She knew that certainly the Holy Spirit was in her because she could not have done what she'd did on her own. If it were one thing she knew, you had to have the Spirit of the Living God living in you in order to handle yourself with dignity in times of disaster. On the way home she decided to listen to the angelic sounds of Sister Crystal Rucker an artist she'd loved from the first time she'd heard her on YouTube. The sister had a way of taking Christine to church and she needed nothing more than to be reminded of how good God is and how awesome His love is for her, the church. As she pulled into the driveway, she noticed that the house glowed. She couldn't make out what was going on because of the heavy drapes, but she felt excitement tingling in her gut.

Before she could turn the knob, the door opened and standing before her was the beautiful earthly king that God had blessed her to be a helper to. She was just about to greet him when he gently took her briefcase and purse from her hand. Then he slowly lifted her in his arms while peering directly into her eyes. Christine, haven't felt this feeling overtaking her body in a long time. He carried her into the kitchen nook and sat her on a stool in front of a candlelit dinner and a bottle of red wine.

"Are you enjoying your dinner darling?"

"Yes Mandery, thank you so much for this."

"No, Christine, I thank you. This is just my way of saying to you that I am so sorry baby. I almost allowed the enemy to entice me with lust, and baby I know that it wasn't of God. I also realize that I've allowed a breakdown in my life and relationship with God and that has no choice but to change. I have this day rededicated my life to Christ Jesus, Christine."

"Oh Mandery! I am so proud of you." Christine said through a stream of tears.

"Christine, I am proud of myself. First, for realizing that I neglected to keep God first, two, for the Lord not allowing me to take things with Sharmen any farther, and three, for God blessing me with a wife like you. Some other woman would have cut a fool and probably even kicked me out, but my wife refused to let the enemy have any place in her life."

"Mandery, please don't think I did it on my own. Baby, the Holy Spirit was my guide and had not He been in operation in my life, I probably would have done something foolish. Baby, I don't want to lose you, but I also don't want to keep you if you don't believe that God put us together. I believe that because God put us together, no man, not even us, can destroy this marriage."

"Wonderfully put Christine. And I know without a shadow of doubt that God allowed me to find you. I will not ever abuse what we have again."

"I know Mandery. Not because you are telling me this, but because the Holy Spirit had already given this to me in a dream. I knew that it hadn't gone any further and wouldn't, and I also knew that God would restore our marriage."

"Praise God! " Mandery yelled while holding up his glass and Christine clicked her glass with his and laughed out, "Thank you Lord."

After dinner, Mandery carried his wife to a garden tub filled with bubbles and roses. He was pulling out all the stops, and this would be a night that she'd always remember. As Christine soaked in the special bath made just for her with her eyes closed, Mandery tenderly caressed her body with the bath sponge. Then he began to kiss her face and rub her hair.

"Christine baby look at me. I want you to know that I do love you, and here is a token of my love." Mandery handed Christine a little velvet blue box and when she opened it, she almost jumped straight out of the tub. It was the four carat diamond ring she'd been secretly eyeing. How did he possibly know? She thought.

"Mandery, how did you know?" She asked in a whisper.

"Baby, I know your heart." He said sounding so sure of himself. Then he reached down and pulled his wife to himself and embraced her in deep love and affection.

Chapter Thirteen

How Does His Wife Feel About The Affair?

Sharmen

Sharmen didn't know how to take what had happened. Here was a woman who seemed to be the very epidemy of strength and probably could have beaten her down, but chose instead to invite her to church. She had never met a woman like Christine, and wasn't sure as to why she'd treated her the way she did. Sharmen decided to go to her mother, and tell her what had happened.

After she'd explained everything to her mother, her mother felt it necessary to just hug her.

"Sharmen, I thank God because that woman could have killed you."

"Momma, I know and had it been my husband, I probably would have hurt her."

"Baby girl, I know this is all you've seen in me. Truth be told, I never wanted my life to be this way. No one ever told me that I was worthy of my own man. Everybody just accepted me being the mistress and I began to accept this for myself. God in heaven knows that I've prayed for you never to get caught up in this kind of relationship, and He has answered my prayer."

"I'm glad someone was praying for me because when I walked in that door, I felt like my heart stopped."

"See, Sharmen, that's the thing with being a mistress. You don't know what will happen if you get caught. What if his wife didn't have the Holy Spirit? I assume that Christ is really truly living in her by the way she handles things, but what if she hadn't been so saturated in God's spirit? Would she have killed you?"

"Mom, I don't know, but what I do know is that I couldn't ever take another confrontation like that. I don't need to know."

"I am so glad. Baby, my best friend Rita was killed, because of a married man. Not only did his wife kill Rita, she killed him, and herself. You see, everybody is not rooted in Jesus Christ. You just don't know what will make a sinner go over the edge. Nothing is stopping a sinner from doing a dreadful deed. I know, I was a *sinner, but thank God I am saved now. I might be living by myself, but I thank God that I am living free from sin. That's all I want for you Sharmen. Don't want a man so much that you will compromise everything you know that is right to do. God doesn't honor that and believe me; He will pull His hedge of protection from around you."*

"I understand mom. I really think that I am going to take Christine up on that church trip. I just need a sister who understands what I am going through. How lonely I feel at night. Maybe, just maybe, God will send me some help, and a man who I can help."

"Baby, God will do whatever you need Him to do if you put Him first in your life. Putting Him first Sharmen means that you live according to His statues and nothing else matters except for your love for Him. Because of your love for Him, you obey Him, and honor Him as your Lord."

"Okay mom. I love you and I'll come back by tomorrow."

"Okay baby, give momma a big hug. You be strong you hear. God knows, and He will provide. I wish my momma would have told me what I am now able to tell you."

180

"Love you."

"I love you too, darling."

There are so many mixed emotions that go on in the mind of a wife of an adulterer. Look at Sarah after she chose to hand her maiden to Abraham. Do you see how she felt? I really want to deal with this situation, because there is no cure to violation. Time is the only thing that heals you.

As with everything I write, because of the unction of the Holy Spirit, I fight about it. Why? I have to tell so much about myself. Some writers are able to leave out their junk but God always uses my testimony to help someone heal. But get this, before I can help, I always have to go through something. You see, it was okay when my first husband was cheating, because I was cheating just as hard as he was. The test comes in when I've decided I don't have to live like that, and then the devil tempts my second husband. Baby, you have to know that the enemy is coming. How? You never know, but you must make the determination stand that "NO WEAPON that is FORMED against YOU (or YOUR MARRIAGE) shall PROSPER."

You've Been Anointed to Fight

God knows everything concerning you, and if you look at the negative in your life as the weapons formed against you, you can take a stand that they won't prevail. So, I figure that every circumstance that I and my marriage go through is but for the kingdom of God. It is but for a testimony to my sisters and brothers that God will work out every wrong in our lives if we love him (Romans 8:28). Whatever demon God allows to enter your territory, is the demon that you are anointed in the Spirit to fight!! This demon concerning adultery, homosexuality, and fornication is mine to fight. This is why I write. To wage war against a present enemy who is trying to siege God's children ultimate blessing...eternal life!

This fight for your marriage, for your children, for your peace is only allowed to enhance and strengthen your faith.

HEBREWS 11:6

"But without faith it is impossible to please Him, for he who comes to God must believe that He is, and that He is a rewarder of those who diligently seek Him."

Therefore, God requires faith in Him that we not only believe that He is, but that we believe that He is involved in every area in our lives. So as we go through, we diligently seek Him for divine revelation that will make us stronger, wiser, and fit to fight for the kingdom. So no matter what we go through, it's for the kingdom of God.

When my husband confessed his calling into the ministry, I made it my business to intensely educate him on how the spirit of jezebel operates concerning God's chosen vessels. I didn't want him to fall into the trap of the enemy and I didn't want to fall myself. I didn't want him to get caught in sexual sin, nor did I want to have to hurt someone. Believe me; I was angry enough to hurt any woman or man who would have tried to come to my husband with sexual persuasion. Why? Because I blamed this on the reason my first marriage failed. And there was still a spot concerning anger in my life that God needed to heal me from. When I first married my second husband, I reminded him that if he ever cheated on me, I would hurt him. Those are powerful words and the enemy wants us to do just what we said.

Well lo and behold, exactly what I feared the most came on us. I woke up one morning from a dream. Here's my dream…

There was a young woman telephoning my husband. Every conversation she was leading up to him going to her house. He was going through spiritual warfare and she was trying to over-power the fear in him. Then I intercepted a phone call between them, tied him up, and cut him until he told the truth. Then I went to her apartment and shot her. All in a dream.

Needless to say, a young woman was calling my husband, and she'd just gotten a new apartment. Don't you know that demons (demonic forces of evil) will tell secrets? It's not so much for the one who is involved, than it is for the one whom the secret is revealed to. The devil was trying to take me out, and he knew just how to do it. Get my husband caught up in anything that remotely felt to me like he was cheating or going to cheat.

I'm here as a wife to let you know that, at the moment a wife finds out she could either loose it or block it out. Either way, she tries to deal with it. Meantime, my dream uncovered some truth and I cut my husband. I ended up with two years' probation, and I thank God for the child who was trying to give herself to him. I know it was the prayers of my grandmother that blocked me from that young lady. God only knows what would have happen.

Danyelle Scroggins

Don't Invade My Life

Invaded is how his wife feels and it's certainly how I felt. One of the worst things a woman can do is put on another woman's underwear. No one wants to share their underwear and neither their husband, which is similar. For me, the going to church, preaching, teaching, and Holy Ghost filled evangelist still had a doormat demon that was ready to kill. I didn't know the extent of the anger in me. I didn't know why I lost all self-control. As I watched my husband lay on my mother's sofa bandage up, I had no pity for him, I beat him some more. My mother had to put me out of her house, and my daddy sheltered over him to keep me from hurting him. Boy! It was like the zookeeper had unleashed the mad tiger. I didn't know that I could be so evil.

I felt like I was before God trying to justify my actions and God was still showing me how so many saints could be destroyed by our actions. I went to our church and laid prostate before the Lord, and I heard the voice of God say..."I've

186

allowed you to go through this storm in order for you to truly be set free from the curse. I allowed Reynard to be blinded so that this demon could sneak up on him but I lifted a standard against the enemy concerning him. I needed you to be familiar with the curse in which I've delivered you from that have been handed down from generation to generation. I have protected you and your children but you must know who I am and who you are in me. I am the Lord thy God which healeth thee."

I cried and thanked God, but I still had no understanding of what He'd just said. A couple of days later, I was watching television ministry and the preacher began to talk about generational curses. As he spoke, I remembered my aunt and biological father telling me of an uncle who was so angry that he killed two of his brothers. I thought, surely, I wouldn't kill my own brother, and God reminded me that I had almost killed someone closer than my own brother...my husband. God desired to set me free. This spirit of anger was laying doormat in my life, waiting on the opportunity and instruction from the enemy to snatch my husband's life, destroy my life, and totally alter my children and our member's lives. The Lord kept me, but unfortunately some weeks later, there was news of a preacher murdered by his wife.

I know enough about the spiritual world to understand that when there's a hit out on you, if you prevail, that demon will keep on until he finds someone weaker. That lady was weaker than I was, but I prayed for her. But God. It was nothing but the power of God that had kept my story from being the same as hers. Had this not taken place, I couldn't truly tell you how a wife feels when her husband cheats. Although my first husband and I battled with infidelity, it wasn't so bad because I wasn't where I am now in Christ Jesus. It hurts, but when you have revenge as an outlet, things aren't as painful; but know that revenge can makes things worse.

This time, my heart was crushed. It was the most painful thing I'd ever gone through. I felt so betrayed and at times used. Then when I took inventory of all the times she'd called my husband, I feel like a fool. It is this very feeling that will make you leery of women and no woman is exempt. I began to question every relationship with any woman that he had. It seemed to become my job, to police my spouse. But my sister, it is so hard to live like this.

He Can't Come In, Unless You Let Him

One night, I was on my way to search his car and when I opened the door, I saw a snake going across my back door step. When it heard me, it started slithering so fast. I hurried and shut the door and immediately God said…

"The enemy can't come into your house unless you let him in. Stop seeking the things of the enemy and seek Me."

From that point on, I stopped searching for mess. I had beaten the enemy by not killing anyone, but then he was destroying my mind. It was now that I finally saw his attack, and decided that the enemy didn't have any place in my life, my heart, or my marriage. I went to the living room and stretched out on the floor and started singing, "I Surrender All." I needed to surrender everything to the Lord. That night, my husband came where I was and said, "I promise you, I didn't have sex with anyone. I don't know how I let this happen to us. All I know is I stop feeling like I was worthy of you. I started feeling like I was too dumb compared to you and I let my imperfections make me desire someone who would see me as great." Boy, was that a load off of me and a slap in the face at the same time. Here, the husband whom I adore standing before me, thinking he's less than the perfect man for me. Now, the healing could begin.

Along with anger management classes, I started researching every scripture known concerning forgiveness. It was a daily activity to remind myself how God forgives, how He has forgiven me, and how I must forgive others. I had to start speaking the Word over myself and my situation. My classes were run by Dr. Meece who was a preacher. He spoke into my spirit... "God allowed you to go through this so you can encourage someone else." It was this very same day that I started writing this book. It was healing for me the mistress, and me the wife. And get this, God allowed me to minister to the very young woman that was preparing herself to be my husband's mistress. I was able to assure her that this time, God was in the program and may not be the second time. It is my prayer that my words are with her even unto this day. I spent so many days repenting. For all the lives and marriages I could have ruined. It was evident that after this ordeal, I was a changed woman.

Women Worthy Of Praise

I thanked God for everything. Even for an aunt who was not ashamed to tell me, "I stayed because of my children, and my love for my husband." I even thanked God for my mother, who had to live through my stepdad having children on the outside. I didn't understand it back then, and instead of having to live her life, I decided that if he cheated on me, I'd cheat on him and this is how my first marriage was governed. Now, I knew better. My cheating wouldn't solve anything. It will only make things worse, and damaged my relationship with God. Now, I saw my mother staying in a different light. Today, my dad is Holy Ghost filled and is an avid church attendee. Who would have ever known that God would work a work in my dad so profound? I now see my daddy as a strong black man. Not because of his not cheating but because of his putting God first and head of his life. When you put God first and head, He'll take care of the mess and the rest.

So I say to my sister, "Bounce back baby girl." The affair wasn't about you in the first place. So many people get caught up, and they don't know why. Sometimes the why is simply that they didn't have a stronger relationship with God. Now, I keep asking God to keep me even when I can't keep myself.

For you nosey folks who enjoys when the preacher or anyone falls, get you some business. Before you start spreading what you heard, pray for those involved. It is hard enough to get through this without folks searching for information to put on blast. God needs some folks who will go down on bending knees for their sisters and brothers. God also needs some folks who will just say, "No!" No, I won't cheat with you. No, you can't bring that woman or man that's not your spouse to my house. No, I won't allow you to bring me into your mess or marriage.

We all handle adversity in different ways. What might not faze you might literally destroy someone else. Before you allow yourself to get caught up, think about how you would feel. The Bible says for us to treat our neighbors as ourselves. That simply means, don't treat anybody anyway that you wouldn't want to be treated.

To those of you who have been affected by an affair and are in limbo wondering should you stay or go…Trust God! Please don't make a decision based on what folks think or have to say. You know your husband better than anyone else. So, you know if he has a problem or if he's just plain ole greedy. Some men take longer to be delivered from sexual sins than women. Sex is a stronghold and you have to be totally surrendered unto the

Lord to be able to resist the devil. Remember this, we can't say what our husbands sins will be; we only know where we fall short. Nevertheless, we do have the authority to break that stronghold from over our husbands with Fasting and Prayer. Hold your head up and walk in victory knowing that you already have won. I refused to carry guilt and shame for someone else's sin or even my own. It won't do you or me any good knowing the details of the affair. The enemy plays with your mind, and will consume you with the what(s), and when(s). Determine within your own mind that nothing can compare to what God has created when it's done how God intended.

It's Just a Stepping Stone

You will not lose your mind. Don't allow the strongholds to take root. Allow the anointing to break every stronghold that is trying to make you captive. Focus on strengthening your relationship with God. There is nothing that a wife can't handle with the help of God. Every milestone that she will face is a stepping stone. God also uses adversity to grow us in our most high faith, and to take us to higher levels in the anointing. You'd be surprised the people that come up to me to touch me so that my anointing will rub off on them. Sometimes, I ask them, "Are you ready for my problems?" Baby I took a whole lot of junk to get the anointing that I have, and the situations and circumstances were right behind the junk. We don't understand what God is doing when we are going through, but He most certainly knows the plan He has for us. I am even anointed to help you flee from the spirit of a fornicator, adulterer, jezebel, and lazy wife syndrome if you want to be. Do you want to be free? Do you want to live free? And I didn't get the ability overnight. I got where I am by going through what I went through. Don't buy your sense…Let me guide you to better sense!!!

So the answer I feel to this chapter's question…How does his wife feel about the affair? Certainly not at the beginning, but after she takes inventory of everything, she still considers herself…BLESSED!

Chapter Fourteen

What Husbands Need To Know

Sharmen

Sharmen made it home and went directly to check her answering machine. She could see the light blinking as an indicator that someone had called. She quickly hit the red flashing button and was so surprise to hear Mandery as her first caller. The machine said, "First call seven a. m." Then there was his voice.

"Hey Sharmen, I just wanted to apologize to you for my selfishness. I shouldn't have kissed you, and I shouldn't have led you on. I am so desperately asking God to forgive me, and I know that I needed to ask you as well. I allowed stuff, well I should call it what it was, and I allowed the lust of my own eyes and mind to take me to a place where God doesn't dwell. All my life, I wanted to be different from my father and somehow, I was about to go the same route. Please forgive me, and know that I know it wasn't your fault. It is my earnest

prayer that God blesses you with someone who can truly love you. Be blessed. "

Sharmen could feel the tears parading down her face. She'd never met a man like Mandery, and she could very well see why Christine had met her this morning. "I wouldn't let anyone try to wreak my relationship with him either." But all in all, she knew she had. Although they took it too far, Mandery had been a great boss and now she'd jeopardized his friendship, her job, and his marriage.

At this point, she knew that she'd accept his apology, but she felt the need to apologize for her own behavior. What is the most surprising is the fact that the woman who'd she learned this behavior from, didn't even want her to go this route. Her mother was so happy that the Lord had delivered her from becoming a mistress before it had even gotten worse. Sharmen could see the joy in her eyes and it was that very look that made her determine to never mess with another woman's husband. After she'd taken her bath she decided to get the Bible. It wasn't often that she read the Word outside of church but tonight, she needed a word from the Lord.

She went to the place her grandmother always told her to go when she felt like the enemy was trying to trap her…Psalm 141 and she began to read.

"Lord, I cry out to You; Make haste to Me! Give ear to my voice when I cry out to You. Let my prayer be set before you as incense, The lifting up of my hands as the evening sacrifice. Set a guard, O Lord, over my mouth; Keep watch over the door of my lips. Do not incline my heart to any evil thing, To practice wicked works with men who work iniquity; And do not let me eat of their delicacies. Let the righteous strike me; It shall be a kindness. And let him rebuke me; It shall be as excellent oil; Let my head not refuse it. For still my prayer is against the deeds of the wicked."

Then she began to pray…

"Lord, I almost allowed myself to practice wickedness and I know this is not of you. Father, I repent of my actions and deeds done in my flesh. Please forgive me of my sins. I know that you are a just God and I know that You require more from me. Teach me how to wait on You. Teach me how to walk in wisdom. Lord, I desire a mate but I don't want to be envious or covetous. I want who You have for me and not what You've blessed someone else with. So, I ask You to

create in me a clean heart, Lord please renew my spiritual man. Most of all Lord, prepare me to be the woman who can stand beside a Godly man. In Jesus name, Amen.

Don't Make Easy Accommodations

First of all, you need to know that you are a husband. That means that you are already connected in the spiritual and natural to one woman, and she should be enough. You need to know, that while there are many women who will overlook the fact that you are already taken, that doesn't make it right that you will accommodate her advances. My grandmother said that if women knew who they truly are, and not accept anything less than perfection, married men would have no one to cheat with. While this is so true, we still understand that there is sin in this world, and the unrepentant sinner has no morals. So, I must remind you mister that the same lines you run down to someone else to cause them to sin, are the same lines that someone is trying to run down to your wife. Now, what makes the difference is always her response; whether or not she believes in her marriage. Whether you are treating your wife right or not, a woman who believes in her marriage is obligated by God to her marriage. She's fixated on the belief that her God can change anything and anybody...whether they want to be changed or not.

So get this, if she stays with you after knowing you've cheated on her, it's because she sees her God in you. Sometimes, you don't even know who you are yourself and God has given her supernatural wisdom concerning you; since we are a little more apt to hear God, because we believe in things that are intangible. Many have believed in God concerning their cheating husbands and have stayed, and God fixed their situations even to the point they were widowed. Believe that, God answers prayers whether you want Him to or not.

Get this scripture and pin it to your brain...

EPHESIANS 5:28

"In the same way, husbands ought to love their wives as their own bodies. He who loves his wife loves himself."

Women understand that people fall out of love, even with themselves. We are our greatest critics when it comes to loving ourselves. So even if you stop loving yourself, let our love help you to find yourself so you can start loving us better. We don't need you to jump through hoops for us; all we want you to do is love us. Stop buying us gifts when you mess up, buy them before you mess up, and maybe we will credit you for what you have already done. One of the first questions a man asks another man's wife is...Is he treating you right? Would it be true for your wife to say, "He treats me like he treats himself"? So understand this, if you don't understand nothing else that I'm about to tell you, your wife is a part of you. If you love yourself, then you should love her. If you don't love yourself, still find a way to love her. Truly loving her will help you build a sense of pride in yourself that will perhaps cause you to love even you.

A Special Movement

I was His Mistress, and as a mistress it was always about what his wife didn't do. Well could it be that she didn't do these things, because you've never appreciated her? It's very hard to keep treating people good that treat you like crap. The Bible admonishes us too but how many of us have truly mastered the humble and turn the other cheek for better advance-ment movement? When you find a wife that has, you better stick with her because you won't get it so easy the next time around.

You wouldn't imagine how many men I have heard say, "I'm staying because of my children. She doesn't mean anything to me but, they mean everything. If it weren't for my children, I would have left a long time ago." What I don't understand is how men think their children feel when they do stay, and cheat on their mothers? How do you think they feel when they see their mother crying or feel her pain? Brother, you are doing more damage to them, than you are helping them. Could it be that you need that woman just as much as you need your children? Stop trying to be honorable before some woman who loves you because of lust, and be honorable to the woman you promised to love until death do you apart!

She's Not the Problem Solver

You don't make the problems in your marriage better by bringing some naïve, heart-broken, impatient, unsaved woman, or man into your equation. Now you have increased the problems. I have seen a man get so frustrated from trying to take care of home and a mistress, until he left both of them. And just like you make excuses as to why you stay out there, women make excuses to let you stay. Your money paying the bills is not a good enough reason for God's daughter to let you stay.

Now, I must go deeper in the spiritual rim of things concerning affairs. See, more than likely the woman who has decided that she'll be your mistress is highly unstable. You might think she's all there but believe me, she's not. When I decided to be a mistress I was selfish, greedy, and a money lover. Brother get this, those are the three most deadly qualities. The Bible warns us about the love of money being the root of all evil, and know that she's not with you because you look so good, or because you can throw down in the bed. It's because you can provide a way for her to either have an easier life, or what she feels is a more fulfilled life; but understand that it's more about her than you. Some of these women are unstable in their minds, brother. They have never felt love, and then you give them a false sense of hope. Many of you are setting yourselves up for death. I speak in the prophetic when I say, "Flee from this relationship. The enemy will use this very relationship to take your life."

You Can't Right Wrong

Nothing done wrong will ever be right. We must start looking at wrong as a setup from the enemy to steal from us, kill us, or destroy us. Some of these women have emotional problems from abusive, sinful, backgrounds and you position yourself as a part of her problems when you lead her into thinking that she is worthy enough to be your wife. You not only put yourselves in danger, you put your wife, and your children in danger. How? Because you don't know which woman you enter into an affair with will go off the deep end. You don't know which one of them will decide to take your life before you decide to let her go. This is a dangerous situation and the devil is at the root of it.

Let's go back to your children. Your money will never be worth more than the time you spend with them. Every time you take time from your family for some woman, you rob your children. Some of my best moments in life were when my dad was out of work. Even though he couldn't back my mother financially, he did all the other stuff like: comb my hair, teach me how to ride a bike, teach me how to count, and carried me to baseball games, to parks, he cleaned, he cooked, he wrestled, and he showed me that he loved us. If it had not been for these moments with my dad, I wouldn't have allowed Dwight to have the relationship with our children that he has. Even after our divorce, I made it up in my mind that I would not use them as a prone to make him obey or do what I wanted. Even when he didn't have the child support, he saw his children. I even took him off child support so that he wouldn't have debt hanging over his head. Because of circumstances, he just couldn't afford to pay the money, but he gave plenty of his time. He taught our children some values that only he could have taught them. I thank God for him as the father of my children.

Men of God you need to know that your children are depending on you. I know that every woman is not like me. Some of them aren't going to take you off child support, and then some of you won't do right if they did. But to those of you who just don't have it, do what you can. It's about the children. I went here because it was on my heart. So many men have divorced, and it wasn't their faults. Some of their wives had that whoremongering spirit and couldn't be satisfied. So no, I don't always agree when the courts take the children and give them to a wife who's decided she didn't want to be married anymore. That's why our children are in the shape they are in. They are their dad's seed, and some other man is nurturing them and sometimes he's of a lesser quality than their dad...not saved!!! So, I don't believe that a woman should be rewarded the child, just because she is their mother. I believe that God has raised some strong men who can nurture and care for their own seeds as if they carried them. I'm not in to preaching what I feel is good, but instead what I know is right.

God says if a man doesn't work, he doesn't eat, and so you are cursed to work. I know that some things prevent this but you must find a way to produce financially that doesn't concern drugs and illegal activity. God will give you in the still of the night a solution to your problems. Just trust God. Just believe God.

Purge! Purge! Purge!

I know that separating yourself from sin is hard. It's not just hard for men; it's hard for women too. You have to pray, and I mean every day. Getting free from sexual sin takes purging; it takes a surrendered heart who knows that they can't break free by themselves. I use to love sex, and didn't know why. After it was over, I still had that same longing that made me do it again. I think God allowed me to go through this so I could help men in this area. It's all in your mind. The addiction of it, the high from it, the accomplishment of it, the enjoyment of it, the satisfaction from it, is all in your mind. Notice the words I used...Addiction, High, Accomplishment, Enjoyment, and Satisfaction. Can you see the lust of the flesh, the lust of the eyes, and the pride of life? (1 John 2:16)

I had to first take a look at the worldly me. I was so caught up in the world, until the things that the world loved became what I loved the most. I believe that we have to confess our faults and sins to be delivered from them. And if you really want to be set free, the Lord will set you free. I earnestly desired for God to make my flesh subject to His Spirit that lived within me. When your flesh become subject to the Spirit of God that's within you, your flesh loses its control over you and your actions. You are no longer governed by what you see, what you feel, or what you think.

NUMBERS 30:2

"When a man makes a vow to the Lord or takes an oath to obligate himself by a pledge, he must not break his word but must do everything he said."

God expects you to honor the vow you made to Him concerning His daughters. If you have a daughter, think about how you expect her husband to treat her. God expects the same thing from you concerning His daughter.

How would you feel if someone mistreats, uses, abuses (physically, mentally, or emotionally), degrades, runs games on, disappoints, mislead, or neglects your daughter? Not too good and I know that God doesn't approve of you doing these things to His daughters. You vowed to protect her, to love her, to keep her, never forsake her, to put her above all others, to honor and cherish her. To do all of this until death separates you from her.

All God wants you to do, is honor your vow. He suffers divorce because of the hardening of our hearts and I need you to know that if your heart is still harden...you won't see God. The Bible says, only the pure in heart shall see God. Don't let someone's earthly mishaps cost you a view of a just, infallible, wonderful, awesome God.

Taking Authority

Men, get a hold of yourselves and come up to where God wants you. You are earthly Kings, heavenly bound. God has created you in His very own image, and His love for you has no bounds. You must put on righteousness, and clothe yourselves in authority. Take authority over everything that concerns you; know the ways of the enemy. Knowledge of how he operates will help you to know him, resist him, and to flee from him. No man goes into battle without first studying his opponent. Put on the whole armor of God so that you won't fall into the set traps which are designed to destroy you.

I heard a man say that all a husband wants is some sex and some food. But all I see in both are ways to quench the flesh. My daddy says, "A Godly man doesn't and can't eat at anybody's table." Simply saying, a Godly man is determined not to allow his flesh to govern him because he has been blessed with one table (his wife's) to enjoy the fruits of his labor.

Danyelle Scroggins

Mandery

When Christine was fast asleep after their romantic evening, Mandery covered her up and quietly kneeled beside their bed to pray. As he stretched his hand towards Christine, he asked the Lord to protect his wife. He asked the Lord to give her every desire of her heart, because she was worthy of them all. Then after he'd prayed for her, he prayed for his daughter. Lord, allow our daughter to be the woman her mother has become. Allow the qualities that she sees in her mother to become the goal at which she'll strive to achieve. Then after he'd prayed for everything concerning his family, he turned his attention towards himself. And Lord, please help me to be the man you've created me to be. I want to be mighty in valor and slow to move. Direct my path and govern my flesh and most of all Lord, please keep me in Your perfect will. Amen.

Chapter Fifteen

God's Daughters

Christine and Sharmen

Christine waited patiently for Sharmen to catch up to her on the sidewalk. She'd hope that Sharmen would show up, and everything inside her leaped when she saw her car coming around the corner. God was going to do a new thing in the both of them. As she waited she thought, who in her right mind becomes friends with a woman who was about to be their husband's mistress. At the same moment the Holy Spirit answered...a true sister.

Sharmen could see the women coming from all different directions headed for the church. She was certain that she would be late, but for some unknown miraculous reason, she'd gotten out of the office at the right time. As she gathered her Bible and tablet she couldn't help but think about Christine. How could she be going to church with a woman whose husband she was trying to take to bed? As soon as the thought came to her mind, the Holy Spirit said…she's your sister and you are forgiven. A tear started trailing down her cheek, and just as she cleared it and looked up, there was Christine standing with her arm stretched out to her.

Christine could see clearly that Sharmen was so heavily in thought that she hadn't even noticed her waiting for her. Then she saw Sharmen wipe a tear from her eye. Christine knew that the devil was probably trying to invade her thoughts as he had tried hers. They were sisters now in Christ Jesus, no matter how they met. God had intended for it to be that way. She made two quick steps and before she knew it, Sharmen was sobbing in her arms…just like a little sister would.

"I'm sorry Christine. I'm just so emotional."

"Look Sharmen, I just want you to know that God is in this. I don't have any ill feelings towards you, and I love you with the love of God."

"Thank you Christine, I needed to hear that. I was feeling guilty for even coming, and I almost turned around."

"That's exactly what the enemy wants but the devil is a liar. He cannot and will not have authority over how you feel. God has forgiven you and so have I. Don't *let his weapons of guilt and shame prosper. God has a word for us tonight and we are going to receive. Okay."*

"Okay." Sharmen said trying to smile through a tissue trail left on her face.

Christine took a handkerchief from her Bible, and gently wiped Sharmen's face free from all the tissue. Then she took her hand in hers and they walked into the sanctuary.

After a dynamic hour of praise and worship God's Spirit was truly working. Women were stretched out at the altar and some were even on the floor between the pews. Sharmen had never witnessed a move of God so powerful. She was so amazed at how freely Christine praised the Lord. She watched her until she found her own place of praise. She'd never said, "Hallelujah" in the church before and now she was crying out with all she had. She desired everything these women had. She wanted the Holy Spirit first of all, and a closer walk with God.

As the women began to gather their composer the Co-Pastor asked the question, "Has God done anything for anybody?" The women lost their minds all over again, and so did Christine and Sharmen. God had spared Christine from having to live with a cheating husband. and the pain behind that and He surely had spared Sharmen for being the type of woman she never wanted to be. So they both in their own minds and hearts had something to be grateful for, and something to go absolutely praise crazy about.

There's one thing that I've found out about being God's daughter. You will go through, but He's on your side. Sometimes you might have to cry, but that's alright too. Your tears become the escape before your breakthrough.

Some of you are reading this book, and wonder why God's daughters stick by their husbands. You wonder why we just don't leave so you can have him. Let me tell you why…

We understand that just because God has delivered us, doesn't mean that our husbands are delivered. We understand that God has put us her to help our husbands meet God in prayer. We are his aid in everything. We also understand that the enemy is on a mission to destroy our husbands daily. We also know, that God will sometimes allow the enemy to put his hands in our situations to bring us closer to Him, and to cleanse us from imperfections. Can I get a witness?

---

1 CORINTHIANS 10:12

"So if you think you are standing firm, be careful that you don't fall."

However, we realize that we are but for the grace of God. We understand that neither one of us is above sin, nor that it is a daily struggle to be free from sin. It is foolish to think we have overcome some things in this life. Therefore, it is our prayer that God keeps us even when we can't keep ourselves. My sisters our sins are not greater than God's faithfulness.

---

1 JOHN 1:9

"If we confess our sins, he is faithful and just and will forgive us our sins and purify us from all unrighteousness."

I believe that God was on to something. When we confess our sins, you can hold us up to the standard of righteousness because you now know our shortcomings. Whereas my husband confessed a spirit of lust, I confessed a spirit of anger. How could I stand in judgment of him when I had my own demons?

JAMES 2:13

"Mercy triumphs over judgment!"

Be angry but sin not was tucked in my memory, but its concepts weren't safely hidden in my heart. God's daughters understand that one of the greatest aspects of being who we are is our ability to forgive like our Daddy (our Heavenly

Father). (I often call my Father, my Daddy because growing up I had some issues concerning my earthly dads (biological and stepdad). Nevertheless, when I became grown, I went to the Lord in prayer concerning these feelings. God shared that no one could Daddy me because He created me differently. I needed to have the affection for Him that a girl has for her dad.) Lots of you didn't grow up with a daddy in the house so I offer you my real Daddy...God the Father, Son Jesus, and Holy Spirit.

MATTHEW 6:14-15

"For is you forgive men when they sin against you, your heavenly Father will also forgive you. But if you do not forgive men their sins, your Father will not forgive your sins.

Our Father has clauses and these clauses require that we do unto others, as we'd want them to do unto us and also that we live according to the things that He has done. We can't afford for our Father to not forgive us for our sins. His not forgiving us could cost us an eternity in Hell. I've never gotten the human concept to not forgive someone, because of what people would think of us. God's daughters don't care about slanders. We know who we are and we forgive because of whose we are. You can't put us anywhere except for out of your life, but if our Heavenly Father put us out of His life...we can't even conceive the thought. Just to write that made me squeamish. We are determined to be more concerned about what our Father thinks about us.

Freedom in Forgiving

You'll be surprised at how free you become when you forgive. Remember the story I told you about earlier...the female that molested me? After I came back home and my divorce was finalized, God began to teach me about forgiving. I had been lying before the Lord, praying for a forgiving heart towards my ex, but God said, "I want to take you deeper." I was working at a counseling center and in walks the woman who molested me. She was a drug addict and an alcoholic and she looked terrible, but I would recognize her anywhere, even in her worst state. She came to the window to ask for some coffee, and she didn't even notice me. It was at that point that I asked the Lord to let me forgive her completely, and to please save her soul.

I haven't seen her since that day, but I knew when she walked out of those doors, I had truly forgiven her and felt so much compassion towards her. God only knows what she went through as a child, and who'd hurt her the way she hurt me. And although Satan meant it for my bad, it would now become my testimony of forgiveness and strength to overcome the enemy. God's daughters forgive in spite of the hurt and pain, because we believe the promises.

We stay with our husbands, since God put us there to hold them up. We hold them up through the good and the bad, with prayers as our guiding light. Baby, I know how to pray. Being married has changed my prayer life so. And through prayer, I have learned how to faithfully love God. When someone exposes themselves, you better understand how they operate.

Through communion with God, I've learned how He operates. He operates through and with love. When you truly learn to love like He loves, you find that love not only covers faults, it helps you look beyond faults. You may see my husband in your light, but I see in a beyond light.

There are benefits to being God's daughter…

- You see clearer, but you still understand that it's not what you see all the time, it's what you believe.

- You stop looking for the world to satisfy you, and to give you what you need; because you know all that you need comes from the Lord.

- You stop trying to fulfill voids with money and men. Nobody can love you like God can, and He's proven it over, and over, and over again.

See I was excepting counterfeits like you. All I wanted was a good man. I thought a good man was a good provider. The devil has a way of trying to make everything about money. If a man gave me money, then he was good. But good doesn't put anybody in heaven. There's nothing like a Godly man. Before you expect God to let you be found by a Godly man, get yourself together.

MATTHEW 7:11

"If you, then, though you are evil, know how to give good gifts to your children, how much more will your Father in heaven give good gifts to those who ask him."

God's love and His gifts don't ultimately cost me my life. His love and gifts are conditional, but the condition is easy. All I had to do was give Him my life. Take the life that already belonged to Him in the first place and chose to let Him lead me, teach me, guide me, instruct me, direct me, and most of all, keep me. Can you see the benefits of being God's daughter?

It's having twenty four seven protection, provision, and instructions to perfection and purpose. I understand that I must be accountable for my actions, and if they aren't to perfect me, or to secure me in my purpose, they don't need to be a part of me. I don't have to answer that I am blessed and highly favored, every time you ask me how I am doing. You see, I am blessed and highly favored by how I love, how I give, and how I live. This is a part of knowing who I am, and who God is to me.

Why would a Daddy put his little girl in a big nasty world without having already made a plan to protect, provide, and care for her?

PSALM 46:1

"God is our (MY) refuge and strength, an ever-present help in trouble."

My God knows that I need His refuge and strength. He knows that my days are full of troubles. What He also knows is that I'm not strong enough to bear some of these things. I'm just not equipped to carry the load. So He urges me to cast my cares and the things that concern me, on Him, because He cares about me.

Do you want to have a Father like mine? You are excepting my Father to make me except you as my sister. I don't see you as the woman who tried to take my husband, or cause me pain. All I see is another one of my Father's daughters trying to get it together. You must understand that you were created for His purpose, and your agenda (because of your flesh) is nothing to Him.

MICAH 6:8

"He has showed you, O man, what is good. And what does the Lord require of you? To act justly and to love mercy and to walk humbly with your God."

He doesn't require much of us and when we meet His requirements, it entitles us to make decisions that seem crazy to others. It entitles us to treat people good when others think we ought to despise them. It entitles us to show mercy to those who need mercy. It entitles us to give Him all the credit and praise for everything He has done in our lives.

The Women Workshop

"Glory to God in the highest. I see by the way the Lord in supping with us that we have some praying women in the house tonight. I don't know why God is taking me here, but I know someone in the house tonight is wondering if God truly forgives them. Does he forgive you for being the harlot? Does he forgive you for making mistakes? Does he forgive you for coveting your sister's marriage? Does he forgive you for that envy and hatred that almost consumed you? Yes He does. Yes, He will. God will forgive you for sins and He desires to forgive you. He's in the building and all you have to do ask Him."

"Hallelujahs!" Began to ring out all over the building.

"He knows what you stand in need of today? All you have to do is let Him have His way today. Give God your full heart, mind, body, and your soul. Do it now!!! Tomorrow just isn't promised, and He wants to dwell in you. Catch your sister by the hand. Come on grab her hand in yours, like she's your very own sister."

"Look her in the eyes, and tell her that God forgives her."

Christine held on to Sharmen's hand and vice versa. They did just as the Co-Pastor had instructed them to do. Then right there in the building, the women started hugging each other. Women were receiving breakthroughs, and nothing was going to stop them from receiving what they came for.

Then the choir started singing…

"I need you, you need me, we're all a part of God's body. Stand with me; agree with me, we're all a part of God's body. It is his will that every need be supplied. You are important to me I need you to survive."

Then the women started coming two by two to the altar for prayer and the Co-Pastor and her team of *intercessors laid hands and prayed for them all. After every woman was prayed for the Co-Pastor said, "Be the best daughters to God that you can be. We are all God's Daughters, and He loves us."*

After the experience was over, Sharmen wrote her home address and phone number down on a piece of paper, and handed it to Christine.

"Christine you are truly God's Daughter, and although I was setting myself up to become His Mistress, I've found out that there is no greater joy than the joy I feel right now. I know deep down in my heart that I too am now God's Daughter."

"You surely are Sharmen, and now tell me, would you have rather been His Mistress or God's Daughter?"

"God's Daughter!" And the two hugged one another with a sisterly hug and laughed gracefully.

For God's Daughters

Most women feel that becoming a wife is about having an in house provider to help with bills, a cure for being alone, or a solution for having sexual relations without sinning. More than often when asked, "Why are you marrying him?" Her answer is one that is typically frightening. "Because I love him and I want to be his wife." When I asked the question, what is a wife, most answered with the answer that they thought was biblically correct, a help meet. What was even more frightening is when I asked, who was the best example of a wife that they know, and many declared that it is the woman in Proverbs 31. Can you agree that almost every woman who has ever heard or read of this woman testifies that she is the greatest? Well let's deal with Proverbs 31 for a while and see.

Who Is King Lemuel?

Lemuel was the given name of Solomon from his mother. His name meant for God or devoted to God. So in this we see that we aren't dealing with just any old mother. His mother was a daughter of Israel with prophetic instructions of the type of woman that her son should have. I know with this information you might not see anything but with this, I was blown away. Why? Any woman in her right mind wants a man whose name or actions signifies that he is for God and devoted to God. To me this certainly qualifies a man as a "good man."

Most women believe that a good man is hard to find, but couldn't be more wrong. It's not for us to find a man and often when we are found by a man, we often don't want him because he doesn't fit the qualities we've decided we wanted in a man. Nevertheless, I need to let you know that when you are found by a man who is devoted to God, this is certainly a good man. So, if it is a good man that you desire, position yourself so you can be found by a Godly man.

Back To Proverbs 31

So here you find a mother giving her Godly son a prophecy of the type of woman he should be finding. Even though they might not word it the same way, you still can find mothers today instructing their sons on the type of woman they are to marry. So in this, I have found the first breakdown in none existent communication between a mother and a daughter. Who is teaching their daughters how to be a wife? So now, you have a man searching for this type of wife, but women who have no instructions of the kind of woman they should be in order to be found by a Godly man.

God Speaks

God said to me, "Women must learn that being a wife is not a trial and error event. I have opened the scriptures for my daughters to gain the characteristics of a wife but who will teach them."

And I immediately said, "Lord if you teach me, I will teach them."

I still wonder why is it that women don't teach their daughters how to be wives. I can assure you that my mother or grandmother never sat down and told me how to be a wife. Neither did my aunts or cousins who were married. It seems to be an unspoken language and they feel that you should automatically know. So as with anything else, I asked God and He spoke into my spirit, "They use to teach their daughters but when they became broken, they stopped."

ISAIAH 61:1

"The spirit of the Lord is upon me; because the Lord hath anointed me to preach good tiding unto the meek; he hath sent me to heal the brokenhearted..."

Brokenness That Blocks

As I conveyed with the Lord, I was in tears because I could feel the pain that women have been through. Have you ever been so broken that you neglected to do what you knew was right to do. While I studied, I tried to take it all in but my mind couldn't help but try to analyze what was spoken to me through Isaiah. Then God made things clear,

"Danyelle look at your life, your grandmother was heartbroken by her first love, your mother, and then you. Your grandmother was devastated and divorced from her first husband, your mother, and then you. Your grandmother had a blissful second marriage, your mother, and now you. In your case it was a generational occurrence. You were all broken. You were taught to love me, live for me, a how to be a Christian, but no one ever taught you how to be a wife."

Some people don't believe in generational curses but I do. I believe that anything (stronghold) that you don't bind (in spiritual occurrence) on the earth, will find its way through your generation. I do not want my girls hurt by their first love and I don't want them to suffer divorces. I have declared that my girls do not have to go through what we went through in order to be found by the man God has for them. That is why I am teaching them what being a wife is about.

A Pure Example

The Spirit of the Lord spoke to me concerning a strand of pearls. I went to get the pearls out of a vase and I examined them to see exactly what God was trying to show me. They were a set of pearls that belonged to my grandmother and they were beautiful. I sat down and began to write what was in my spirit about the pearls.

Notes about Pearls

Color

Pearl White, Pure

Form

Circles, Well Rounded, Held Together

Quality

Expensive, Costly

Looks

Beautiful, Pretty

Buyers

Exquisite, Well Dressed

After making these notes, I began to compare the pearls with a woman. I gathered that a lot of the qualities and characteristics that the pearls had, women have also. Then I was compelled to take a deeper look at the pearls. I noticed that the pearls had been broken. There was a small piece of wire holding the two ends together. As soon as I tugged, the wire unwrapped and there the pearls were broken before me.

God said, "To you your sisters look good, they seem purified, well-rounded, seem like they're holding things together, they seem to have value, good looks, some of them seem wiser with age; this is what you see Danyelle. I see hurt and heartaches that have led to filthy unpurified lives. My daughters have become cursed carriers, money lovers, mean-spirited, back-bitters, perishing women who are broken before me."

"Oh God," I cried.

Then the Holy Spirit said, "There is an even greater problem. The Word is being blasphemed because of disobedience. I told the aged women to be holy, not false accusers, not drunkards, teachers of good things; that they may teach the young women to be sober, to love their husbands, to love their children, to be discreet, chaste, keepers at home, good, obedient to their own husbands, but this, my daughters have not been honored."

I immediately turned to Titus and there it was.

Brokenness is causing God's daughters to neglect teaching the young daughters the way. A broken marriage in which you did all you felt you could do as a woman, will cause you not to want to teach a young woman how to clean house, cook for her husband, take care of the home while he's at work, or the other wifely duties. A cheating husband will make you not want to teach a young woman to love her husband. Struggles in finances will make a woman not stay at home to clean or cook but take a full time job outside the house. Our inability to resist the enemy has caused so many break downs within the ministry of marriage and in the woman until it seems less than important to be a wife or to teach others how to be a wife.

Brokenness is a spirit that is not of God. Brokenness is that hurt you experience that you just can't seem to forget about and that's keeping you from forgiving. Some of you have experienced some horrible, hurtful things but I speak to you today in the prophetic and say, "God's daughters you are healed in Jesus name."

Is This You?

Does one or any of these statements apply to you? Or have they applied to you at one point in time in your life?

- That man was with me for ten years and he married a girl he only knew then days.

- He got another woman pregnant while he

was living with me and her baby and my
baby are the same age.

- Our divorce was final on Wednesday and he was married an on his honeymoon by Saturday night.

- I found out on our wedding day that he was already married.

- He didn't even bother to show up on our wedding day.

- He has been sleeping with his ex-wife the whole time we were married and was lying about it.

- My husband beat me in front of the kids and the same night, he wants to have sex.

- I go to work every day and my jobless husband rides around in my car and picks up other women.

- My husband is the pastor and he just got caught sleeping with his deacons' wife.

After you've experienced some of these hurts and situations, it hard to tell anyone anything about being a good wife. As a result of these actions that led to brokenness, there are women living as adulterers, liars, fornicators, lesbians, murderers, drunkards, haters, and living dependent of drugs. Some of them can't even trust or love God. Why, because they blame God for allowing them to suffer some of these heartaches.

Daughters, if you live a life channeled by brokenness, you will not only destroy your life, but the lives of the people around you including your children. Some of you are even functioning through a spirit of brokenness as you read this book, but the good news is, it is a spirit. Any spirit that is not of God can be cast out if you want it to be.

Prepare Me To Be Found

Fitted clothes, breast, big butts, long weaves, pretty nails, costly jewelry, and straight teeth, are not the areas in which we will be working on.

239

Your outer appearance has nothing to do with you being found. Don't get me wrong, a sister with a big butt might catch his eye, but I guarantee you that it won't keep him with you. The way you dress, smell, and the money you have might entice him but I promise you, it won't keep him.

Your being found is not based on your ability to get a man, but on ability to spiritually connect with a man. Although, we would like to make it a physical connection, it is not. God did the supernatural in creating Eve from Adam's rib and this formed a spiritual connection between the two of them. She was a part of him. God used divine instructions to form the connection between Hosea and Gomer. God used the lack of submissiveness and disobedience to break King Ahasuerus and Queen Vashti up. God used divine intervention to bring King Ahasuerus and Esther together.

Relationships are not woven together by beauty or charm, but by God. If you fear God and walk in His statues, He will cause you to be found at the right time, in the right season. Now when we enter into quick fix marriages (marriages that we enter into without God to run away from problems), they cause us to suffer heartaches as if they aren't of God. God will even sanctify your quick fix marriage if you both put it in His hands. Why? Once a relationship is formed in covenant and established, it becomes a God thing when we put His Word on it. That's the kind of God we serve. He will allow us to make our own messes but once He has our permission to become a part of it, He will.

If your quick fix marriages turn out to be a total disaster, God will let you remain in whatever condition you are in until you decide that you have had enough. See, God gave man dominion over everything in the earth and you even have dominion over your own situations and choices. If you choose to handle the circumstances of your life without the help of your Heavenly Father, He will let you. That's why 1 John 1:9 says, "If you (yourself) confess your sins (take action towards God for reconciliation), He is faithful and just to forgive you of your sins (then He reacts).

God's reaction is always most definitely based upon your actions. God won't direct your path until you acknowledge Him. God won't heal your land until you humble yourself, pray, and turn from your wicked ways. God won't prepare you to be found by your husband until you ask Him to.

When I decided to let the King get in my business and be the Father to me, His daughter, He placed a spiritual sign on me that read...This daughter is under construction; do not tamper with her!

My same dimples and bow legs that caused men to holler at me, seemed invisible to the eyes. I couldn't even pull an unattractive guy. This is truly when I found out that it wasn't about the physical but about the spiritual. God was doing a spiritual transformation on me and He wasn't going to allow it to be tampered with by physical lust and attraction.

Find The Examples

There are some virtuous wives among you. As you wait, you need to surround yourself with some of these women. Is she is a good wife, she probably has a lot going on but it won't hurt you to jump on her agenda and take the ride along with her.

When I was waiting to be found, I talked to my next door neighbor a lot. Her husband had gotten caught in the devil's web and was doing time in jail. That didn't detour her at all. She maintained her household. She never cheated and she kept her relationship with the Lord. I was compelled by her faithfulness to him, even though he'd gotten caught up in sin. She was her husband's wife no matter what he had done, or where he was. Then I would think about how my grandmother was so dedicated to her husband. How they would sit down and sort out their bills together. How he would drive her everywhere she wanted to go. Even though, she didn't cook, he maintained a clean home and he didn't mind cooking.

She was a praying wife; dedicated to God first and then her husband. Then I'd watch my uncle Bobby and his wife Dell. How they would ride around together like they were each other's best friend. How they laughed at one another and vacationed. How they managed to stay together for so many years. My Aunt Dell worked, but she still came home after long hours, cooked, and took care of her home.

I remembered how my mother would cook a full meal for us and have it on the stove when we got home from school. She worked but at night, you'd wake up and find her cleaning up the house. How she always took care of us and made sure we looked nice. How she'd forgiven my step father for having children outside of their relationship.

When I was younger and married, none of the things I just wrote excited me. In some of them, I saw a crazy woman. Who works all day and come home and cook? Who forgives a man who's had children on the outside? Now, I understood why and how they did what they did, now that I was single and longing for what they had. God was helping me to analyze the examples of His daughters that had been placed before me. There had truly been some virtuous women in my life, and those who had the qualities of Solomon's mothers' wishes of a woman for him. What I'd seen all my life became relevant and that's all I'm trying to tell you. Allow the things you've seen in good marriages help you.

What I Teach My Girls

God will allow you to be found but it's not for the sake of you just saying that you have a husband. God will give to you a husband that will be able to assist you on your Christian journey and you likewise. The bible says, in Matthew 18:19, *"Again I say unto you, that if two of you shall agree on earth as touching anything that they shall ask, it shall be done for them of my Father which is in heaven."*

I believe that God gives you someone, through marriage, to aid you in agreement, as you come before His throne asking for anything upon this earth. When I have a husband, I don't have to call for my mother to touch and agree with me, my husband is there. See, I believe that spouses are to aid one another on this life journey and help usher one another into close relations with the Father. That's why it's important who you marry. How can someone that doesn't believe in God, help me go before His throne? This should be God's daughter criteria for being found...that the man who finds them knows the Lord Jesus Christ as his personal Savior.

I also tell them to be in position. While they are out looking for a man, the man that is for them might not find them because they are out of position. You have to be in position with the will of God for your life in every aspect. If God tells you to go to Lake Bethel, why are you still at Greater Zion because momma nem are there? Get in God's will for your life. Momma has her life and if she's in God's will, hers should be rather decent. Now it's time for you to do as God tells you. Position is everything for God's daughters. God has a specific timing, and place for us and we must be where He has told us to be, when He told us to be there.

Almost Missed My Boaz

Unlike Ruth, I was so hard headed. God sent His chosen man to invite me to his church three times, and I failed to go. I had no intentions ongoing when I finally did go. It wasn't that I had anything against him or his church. I just didn't like the thought of riding for an hour just for Sunday service. Do you see what I am talking about? God had the man with whom I'd have an outstanding partner to come before His throne with and I almost missed the mark because I was too lazy to drive an hour. Do you know that there are so many of God's daughters without what they desire or have prayed for because of laziness?

I almost missed the man that would become my very best friend because of disobedience to the man of God. So don't always think that God is going to drop direction into your spirit during your prayer time. Sometimes He speaks through His men and women. God led him to come to me three times, and three times I failed to obey. I truly thank God for giving me another opportunity that I almost passed on again.

Money and Sex

Don't let money and sex determine who you'll spend your life with. Men have learned that money makes most women move but not God's daughters. We understand that we are not whoremongers and that money does not define who we are or what we do. Look at the King's mother; she tells her son "Give not thy strength unto women" The word strength in the Hebrew is Chayil, which means riches, substance, and wealth. See, men use money to get sex (even back then), so this is the first thing she advises him against. Then she warns him against drinking and she clearly states that when a man is drunk, he forgets the law and his judgment become perverted. How many men do you know have gotten drunk and slept with a woman whom if he weren't drunk, he would have never touched her?

Look at Lot.

So in Proverbs 31:1-9, we see a mother's instructions that will build her son's character and keep him in the way of godliness and righteousness, so that he can be complete in the administration he's in. Being that she knows that it is the man that finds a wife, she asked him in verse 10, "Who can find a virtuous woman?" Is it an educated man or a rich man? No, I believe that this mother way saying that if you remember who you are in character as you are kept in the ways of godliness, then you can find a woman who can co-exist alongside of you and she will possess the qualities in which I am about to tell you about.

She is priceless! See, as God's daughter, you are priceless. There's nothing better than a woman who knows her worth. A woman of worth understands that no amount of money in this world can buy her. She's secure in the fact that happiness and completeness comes entirely from the Lord and she does not want a man to complete her, but she wants to be a compliment for him. That's why his heart trusts in her. He knows that her actions are a compliment of her love. Everything she buys is complimentary to the cause of the life they've established. He doesn't have to worry about her spending their last to get her hair and nails done. He trusts that she will spend wisely and weigh the needs of the family verses her wants. That's why he doesn't have need for spoil, crooked money; get rich quick scams, pyramids, gambling money, or dishonest money.

God's daughters don't put pressure on their husbands in order to keep up with the neighbors or her friends. She's satisfied and content in the things that her husband have provided for her. She appreciates him working daily and she does good towards him because of his provision, protection, and love towards and for her.

What Does Virtuous Mean?

Virtuous is a word that we use often and especially in the church setting. What is so surprising is that most women who've heard the word have never found out exactly what it means. Virtuous means having moral integrity and chaste.

Well what does moral integrity and chaste

mean? Moral integrity is having moral goodness or righteousness and chaste is not having sexual intercourse with anyone except your husband.

God's daughters are good, righteous, and chaste and it's that simple. As His daughter, you have the responsibility of making sure that when people think of you, they think on these three words above.

How Do I Get To This Point?

By first making up in your mind that you desire to be God's daughter, then it starts by first letting go of your past. Do you really know what damage can be done to your mind when you continuously think on the hurtful things that have happened years ago?

PHILIPPIANS 4:8

"Finally, brethren, whatsoever things are true, whatsoever things are honest, whatsoever things are just, whatsoever things are pure, whatsoever things are

lovely, whatsoever things are of good report; if there be any virtue, and if there be any praise, think on these things."

The writer is simply saying that if there is any goodness in you or anything worthy of praise, your mind should be filled with the things above. No one whose mind is cluttered with junk can function in goodness. More than likely revenge, hate, malice, and curses is the elements you function with when your mind is filled with junk from the past.

Rechanneling your thoughts is imperative to having a life as God's daughter.

Once, you've let go of all the hurtful stuff, you can move towards expectations of what is to come as God's daughter. I believe that we dedicate our children to God, our lives to our spouses, but before you get to either of these, why not dedicate your body to the Lord?

In order for God's daughters to operate in the gifts of His Spirit and through total love, you must give your body and your soul to the Lord. Chastity is a way of saying to God that I am remaining free from sex on the grounds that my body belongs to you until you present it to one of your sons. This keeps you free from spiritual wickedness and it causes your ears to be open to God's voice and your mind receptive of God's will. Then you become adamant about forming a deep relationship with the Lord. Learning how to effortlessly fear and reverence God.

Then you'll start to really know your worth. As you began to know your worth, you'll begin to pick your task wisely. You'll become a good steward over your time, money, and every aspect of your life. You'll respect the time that you spend with the Lord and you'll create time to spend with Him no matter how hectic your surroundings become. For those of us who have husbands and children, we should maintain a vigorous desire to always find time to spend with the Lord. Whether it's late at night when everyone is asleep, or in the restroom on our breaks at work. We must always have time to commune with our Father. This is the key to bringing and keeping you at the point of goodness, integrity, and life as God's daughter.

About the Author

Danyelle Scroggins is the Pastor of New Vessels Ministries in Louisiana and the author of three fiction works: Not Too Far Gone, Destiny's Decision, & Evonta's Revenge. Danyelle loves to hear from you, her readers! Feel free to contact Danyelle via her website www.danyellescroggins.com or follow her on Facebook.com/danyellescroggins.

Other Books by Divinely Sown Publishing

www.divinelysownpublishing.com

 Not Too Far Gone

 Destiny's Decision

 Evonta's Revenge

 The Truth Set Me Free!

www.ingramcontent.com/pod-product-compliance
Lightning Source LLC
Chambersburg PA
CBHW051950090426
42741CB00008B/1331